2:7

THE AWAKENING OF LOVE

ANGELA AILEEN GRANT

ISBN-13: 978-1478386193
ISBN-10: 1478386193

Cover design: Ricc Rollins Media
Photography: Vincent Johnson

To: Summerlyn

Thanks for your support!

I really appreciate you!

Practice Thanksliving
Everyday!

Angela
Grant

DEDICATION

This book is dedicated to all those who have ever loved.
Hopefully, that includes you.

Table Of Contents

ACKNOWLEDGMENTS

"Let us be grateful to people who make us happy." –Marcel Proust

As I struggled, just about every day, with deciding to write this book, God would whisper to my spirit that this book isn't about you it is about the people you will help. Thank you Lord for putting it all in proper perspective!

I am grateful for my mom and dad, Sandy and Bob Grant, for being strong enough to watch their baby girl grieve and grow into a new woman. I'm very appreciative of my brother, Robert Grant, Jr. for supporting me and praying for me. Joy, for without your love there would be no book. GG and the Miller families thank you for still considering me to be a part of your family. Nicole, thank you for listening and allowing me to see the upside of my grief. Uncle Richard, thank you for providing me with a get- away trip! To all of my family and friends thank you for your love, support, and prayers throughout my entire life. May God bless you and keep you all. Rex Hauck, thank you for helping me to give new life to my story. Dr. Veronica Walters, thank you for helping me to give birth to this project! And Will thank you for giving me another opportunity to love. I am truly blessed!

"Tis better to have loved and lost than to have never loved at all."

-Alfred Lord Tennyson

FOREWORD

Loss experienced at any time is an unwanted visitor to each of us. At this time in history, we are made to know the daily losses of strangers in all areas of our world and our lives. We feel the sadness of parents of dying soldiers; of children for lost parents and of wives and husbands living out brief loves...too brief. We share the pain of starvation, rape and killing of innocent people around the globe. We know in depth the statistics of degradation and defeat suffered by millions printed and broadcast in unacceptable numbers everyday as we question these stories, disbelieving, in shock and wonder.

What can we tolerate?
How can we respond?
What can we do?

Early on, *The Awakening of Love* tells the close and intimate story of Angela and Dion; their personal perfect love. Hopefully, each of us can find kindred moments as we also, have been touched by another person. We are happy for the friendship they build step by step, honoring the desires and acknowledging the foibles of each as they make their way separately and more and more together.

Many warm memories return from reading their story because, in the descriptions, before final vulnerability rushed into their world, I could trace romantic revelations of my own life. I was engaged at 21 to my fiancée Stacy who was 26. Both Dion and Stacy had the wisdom and tremendous faith of youth, and both were victims at 26. We all had the expectation of perfection; the promise and certain knowledge of unending love assured in emotional physical presence. We touched each other. It was real.

We were bursting with the loves we shared, invincible in that reality. We were blessed! We were beautiful! We were two people in love! Our love was returned in glowing unity. We spoke and no one else was in the room; we smiled and teased, we breathed and mirrored. We were captivated by the wonder of choosing each other. I remember and I cherish.

Each moment together reduced any solitary doubt. Each shared moment supported our agreement that we were given more then we could ever have asked for. One touch, one look assured us, he and I, that we were together in this life. Then, in one unbelievable moment, he was taken away; taken from me. It was not his speech of promise that I missed most but his touch; his reassuring touch which I would no longer experience, I would no longer trust and I could no longer reach for.

I know that loving Stacy sustains and keeps me and allows me to love others. This love, this opening is a location of certainty which can never be turned back, never be denied. God, the Goodness of Life, has given this to us; has entrusted love to us through life itself. We have loved and we cannot take it back. This love, this certainty is not ours alone; we didn't experience it alone and we don't contain it alone. This love is only to be shared, to be affirmed with others; to be lived in giving and ideally, receiving the same moments in time.

As Angela and Dion knit their lives together, step by step, each let down the mask lived behind, choosing to reveal the expressive, momentary and real face which they wished to share with each other. As we turn a page, their experiences remind us of someone who has truly loved us. To lose this person, with whom we are ourselves, is heart-breaking. Our hearts cannot be stitched back together again; cannot be repaired to appear as the same hearts. Our hearts are different; deepened, softened, never again to be closed, contained or kept only to ourselves. When our hearts have learned to care, we cannot go back. We carry loving and this is the journey that Angela describes in her writing.

Angela and Dion's story has again, reminded me of these gifts received. The doubts of being on time to work, arguing rights, being forgotten by a friend, pale in this remembrance. I am beloved, an initiated person in the wonders of love which all of us have experienced big or small; some time or long time with family, a friend, a guide.

We are touched by her writing because we know the truth of what she says. Her experience is singular yet universal because our hearts know it and that is why its beauty is real.

And we can take these caring actions; we can respond beyond bearing the pain of death, we can offer love in circles radiating out, touching those who cry, with our own open hearts.

Lynne Zuckerman, D. Min.
Berkeley, California

"I implore you, daughters of Jerusalem, do not stir up, or awaken love, until it so desires."

Song of Songs 2:7 (KJV)

PREFACE

When I was a young girl, I had a few favorite books with more pictures than words. The stories were standard childhood fairytales with princes and dragons and happy endings. The idea that a frog could become a prince and that a prince could awaken a sleeping princess with only a kiss fascinated me.

I read the books until the pages were dog eared and tattered. Somewhere along the way, I got the notion that I wanted to write my own book. I made a few attempts, but my characters couldn't seem to make up their minds about just where the story was supposed to go.

In college, I continued writing by journaling. I recorded the events of my life, my dreams and disappointments, in a series of bound books. I would also write down scripture from the Bible and inspiring quotes. I even included some poetry. My journals were my refuge, a sanctuary. My words were sometimes also my prayers. My journals made my conversations with God more intimate and specific.

Maybe, I thought, these journals might turn into a story; maybe even a story about a prince or true love, though I had come to believe that neither existed in the real world. I liked reading about romance and relationships, but I avoided them in my own life. All I had to do was look around at the heartache and frustration of my friends in love to resolve never to go down that road myself.

And then, after college, I did fall in love. Seriously, head over heels, forever in love with a guy who was as far from a knight in shining armor as any man could be. But like the kiss in the fairytales, love has a way of transforming people. It changed me and it changed Dion, the man I love.

It wasn't all easy. We brought a lot of issues and ghosts and high expectations with us. We argued. We broke up more than once. Through it all, something kept us coming back together. Call it fate, true love, soul mates, whatever term works for you, all I know is that through the arguing and the making up and hanging on, we passed some kind of threshold where we found our commitment.

Dion proposed to me in a lopsided, loveable, completely unpredictable way. I was thrilled. Lazy weekends were spent planning our wedding. Despite my parent's objections, I moved to Florida to be with him while he finished school. There were mornings I pinched myself, life seemed too good not to be a dream and then I got a phone call.

The voice at the other end, Dion's mother, told me that Dion had been in an accident. I rushed to the hospital. The doctors had done their best but Dion's life was slowly slipping away.

I was in shock. I needed to do something but if this team of doctors and nurses could not save him, what could I do? Friends gathered at the emergency room. We waited together as Dion's strength slowly faded. A hospital chaplain stopped to offer his sympathies and I knew what I wanted to do. I asked the chaplain if he would marry me and Dion. He told me that he could but that no court would consider our marriage legal. That didn't matter to me. I wanted to say the words out loud. "I take you, Dion." I also wanted my heart to hear them.

Dion was twenty-six years old the June he died. For a long time, a part of me wanted to die, too. There were dark days when I thought about how I might end my life. I wondered what loved ones left behind would think or say. Friends and family tried to comfort me but usually only made things worse. Nothing felt the same without Dion. I had been baptized when I was ten years old and I felt that my relationship with God was strong. I had never imagined that there would be a time in my life that I would not want to converse with God until that happened.

A grief counselor suggested that I let my journaling be a release valve for me. I took her advice and let my emotions flow into words onto these pages. In the privacy of those pages, I railed at a God who would take Dion from me. The blackness in my soul stained the pages with words of rage and loss. I was hurt and I blamed God for hurting me.

It took some time before I could acknowledge that I was still thankful for all of the blessings with which He had entrusted me. I see now that being mad with God was a critical part of our relationship. It shook up my faith and made me consider it again not as a child but as a responsible adult.

When I had emptied myself, arriving at rock bottom, I discovered the nothingness I feared, was actually peace. I also found that the God I had abandoned had not abandoned me. I know now that God was carrying me especially through the darkest of times because there was no other way that I could have made it.

Over six years have passed now since the accident. Life isn't better, it's different. There was life with Dion and now, life without him. I'm learning to adjust. Most days there is more light. Breathing in seems a little easier, a little deeper with the passage of time.

I realize that Dion's life and his death were a gift to me from a loving God. That sentence can't explain the distance I had to travel to come to that understanding. My journals became a kind of map, a guide that led me out of the depression and pain.

As a symbol of our love and commitment, Dion gave me an engagement ring. After his passing, I wore my engagement ring and wedding band on my left ring finger. It took me a year and three weeks to take them off but something inside me knew it was time to hold Dion in a different way. I put the wedding band on my right ring finger and I put the engagement ring on a necklace.

As I began to write this book, I put both rings on my right ring finger as a sign of my commitment. In a real sense, I am married to this project and my vow is to honor Dion, and myself and our courage to love. My hope is to share my story with others, so that they might see that even the darkest night ends and that love survives.

Even though I have lost Dion in this world, I am now capable of more love and more joy for having known him. Even though I've lost the man, the room he made in my heart remains.

There are still days that I sit and cry and wonder what it would be like if Dion were still here with me. I am sure that I would not be the woman I am today without having him in my life.

My belief in God leads me to believe that we as his children are being tested. The test is not to hurt us but to see how we are able to deal with the tragedies of life. He gives us tests that he knows we can handle but how we handle the test is up to us. So instead of thinking "Why me," I try to remember that God trusted me with this passage and must really have a lot of faith in me. Even though it did not feel like a compliment at first.

Journal Entry

Why do fairytales always begin with 'once upon a time' when what the writer is really is saying is 'never in time' has this really happened. What the writer and the story imply is that the fantasy could come true, someday, maybe...

For me, I've come awake in a dream. Standing in the ante room of the chapel...Friends and family are gathering. Outside the curtained window, I can see a line of cars pulling into the parking lot.

Two girlfriends are helping me dress. The white of my gown contrasts with the blue of their bridesmaid dresses. One friend places the veil on my head. I look in the mirror. I can touch the mirror but not my image, shrinking further and further from my hand the farther that I reach.

A hand on my shoulder turns me from the mirror. I'm facing the ` sanctuary doors of the church. The doors open. The pews on both sides are filled with guests who turn to look at me as the bridal march begins to play.

My right foot starts forward, instinctively, taking me down the aisle. As I walk, I look toward the front of the church. The minister is there smiling at me. My mother and father, in the first row are gently crying.

I look for Dion, imagining him in a black tuxedo and smile, but he is not there. In his place, on the preacher's left, is a casket. This is Dion's funeral, not our wedding. I am not saying "I do." I'm saying "Goodbye."

I walk past tear stained faces, hoping that the veil hides my own sorrow. Each step brings me closer to a pain I cannot survive, but I cannot stop walking, and I cannot wake up.

"Love takes off masks that we fear we cannot live without and know we cannot live within."

-*James A. Baldwin*

CHAPTER ONE

Masking Emotions

I was never a very good student. I got good grades but was seldom engaged by the subject matter or the teachers. My junior year in High School, however, I took an advanced Language Arts class at the insistence of my guidance counselor. She thought it would look good on my college transcripts. The material was complex, and often boring, but I did my best to at least look interested. Midway through the fall semester, as I daydreamed at my desk, the teacher called my name to read a poem by Paul Lawrence Dunbar titled We Wear the Mask.

I walked to the front of the room. The palms of my hands were a little sweaty as I flipped through the book for the right page. I looked out at the faces staring up at me, cleared my voice and started to read. A moment later, I wasn't aware of anyone else in the room. The words I was reading seemed to have been written specifically about me.

> *We wear the mask that grins and lies,*
> *It hides our cheeks and shades our eyes,—*
> *This debt we pay to human guile;*
> *With torn and bleeding hearts we smile,*
> *And mouth with myriad subtleties.*
> *Why should the world be over-wise,*
> *In counting all our tears and sighs?*
> *Nay, let them only see us, while*

We wear the mask...

I felt this poem in my bones. I identified with hiding my real feelings and smiling through pain. It was what I did. I hadn't suffered any major personal losses. My parents loved each other. My primary family members were still living and I'd been careful with my own heart but I had inherited a severe caution around any emotion.

Tears, to me, were a sign of extreme weakness. The lamentation that always followed any temporary joy my friends found in relationships firmly cemented the walls of my emotional fortress. Each day, I put on my mask and became an actor in my own life.

The only place I was really honest with myself was in my journals. The only place I let my mask down, was late at night, in my room, as I let my emotions and ideas flow onto those pages.

Journal Entry

There is so much more depth in me that you cannot see. You do not know what is inside me. You don't know what tears left the windows to my soul open for me to find out who I really want to be. Unless I invite you to know me, you will not know me.

I like it that you don't try to figure me out. You leave me alone in my aloneness and don't even think of calling me lonely. I'm so happy when it's just me.

I'm not ready to love you because you're not ready to love me. Is anyone ever truly ready to love? Are they sure they can put up with the pain and confusion? I'm not.

CHAPTER TWO
Imaginary Love

High school passed quickly even for a semi-disinterested student. Still there was no question for me as to what came next. My brother and my parents had gone to traditionally black colleges and I wanted to carry on that tradition. I applied to four schools but Clark Atlanta University was my first choice.

My acceptance letter arrived in March of 1998. I was incredibly excited for about ten seconds and then anxiety came crashing in. I was ready to leave my parents' house, but was I ready to live on my own? What was this new life going to entail? Could I survive a college curriculum? I prayed to God that He be with me and help me not to be so nervous.

When my parents dropped me off at on the Clark campus five months later, I remember telling them, "I am about to get my learn on." They thought that was funny.

I settled into my freshman year, learning the campus layout, taking classes and making new friends. And then against all of my own internal rules, I made the mistake of acquiring a boyfriend. My plan for college had been study hard, graduate with honors and no boyfriends. Somehow I ended up with one.

He went to Morehouse College, which was right next door to Clark Atlanta University. I was on his campus as much as I was on my own. I had known him before college but we became friends and eventually boyfriend and girlfriend. The relationship lasted three months. I'm not sure why I let it go on that long. I

9

remember feeling like I was his constant cheerleader and when it was his turn to cheer me, he evaporated.

When I broke up with him it was over the phone during Winter Break. I told him that I really didn't want to be in a relationship my first year in college. He accepted my decision and I thought I heard a twinge of relief in his voice as he said his final "good-bye."

Despite this failure to sustain a real relationship, I carried on an intimate correspondence with the man who only existed in my dreams, at least for now. I found comfort in knowing that at the end of the day my journal would be waiting for me. In that private place, I was allowed to share my dreams and confess my fears. I questioned over and over just what love was. I knew that God was love, but what did love look like in Angela's eyes.

Journal Entry

I want to write of my feelings for you but I'm not sure of what they are. I know that you make me smile whether we're together or apart. I know that I like to laugh with you because I love to see you smile.

I want to hold you. I want to kiss you. I want to love you. I want to make love with you, but I must know you more and want you to know me too. I want to share my dreams with you and make your dreams come true. I want to make you happy.

The day I fall in love with you, I want to make sure it shows in my eyes. I want you to feel it in my kiss. I want to love you. Yes; it is a scary thing, this love. Crying, laughing, singing, dancing and doing them all at the same time. My joy would be to look into your eyes and be able to feel the love you have for me. When that happens, man, you've got me forever.

CHAPTER THREE
A Line Like No Other

I graduated from Clark Atlanta in 2002 with a degree in Early Childhood Education. I wasn't quite sure what my next move would be until my father called to tell me that I either needed to get a job or move back home. I was almost twenty-three years old and not about to move back home which provided strong motivation to find a job.

I started work at a day care center as a Pre-K teacher a week later. My class was comprised mostly of black children. I had a few white students and two Hispanic students, Jose and Juanita, who were fraternal twins.

One day we were doing a lesson about farm animals. In the coloring center, I had crayons and markers and paper. I sat down and drew a cow. Jose sat down beside me and picked up the same color marker and drew his own cow. I took the marker back and drew a pig. He picked up a pink marker and drew a pig that would have made Walt Disney proud. Then I asked him, "What else might you see on a farm." By this time we had an audience of other four and five year olds.

He thought for a minute and then blurted out, "A monkey."

"Monkey! On a farm? No, not a monkey, think again," I urged him.

He thought another minute, and then said, "A dog."

"Sure a dog can be seen on a farm," I replied. We both proceeded to draw pictures of dogs, even though mine looked very similar to my cow. It was one of my first favorite moments as a teacher. I had a breakthrough with this child and he looked so happy.

Not only did I connect with the children, I became close with some of the staff at the school and was invited to the 60th birthday of one of the other teachers. They were going out to a club to celebrate. I was reluctant to go. This crowd was much older than I was but I figured I could make it an okay evening by persuading my cousin, Charys, to go with me. It took some convincing but I finally got her to come along by telling her there would be a lot of guys our age there.

I picked her up and we drove across town to the club. Charys and I got to the front door and could see that the place was packed. It was also blatantly obvious that we were, by a couple of decades, the youngest people in the place.

"Lots of guys our age?" Charys questioned me.

"All these guys were once our age," I said motioning to the aging Romeos prowling the dance floor and bar.

"You owe me one," Charys said but waded in by my side to find the birthday party anyway.

We found them at a table near the dance floor. Hugs and kisses erupted when they saw me. I introduced my cousin and we sat down. Drinks were ordered, and re-ordered and the normal birthday jokes and stories circled around the table.

The lounge was packed and our waitress overwhelmed. I volunteered to go to the bar for refills. I made it around the dance floor only being hit on twice. Leaning on the dark oak bar, I waved down the bartender and ordered rum and coke and a beer. I had to repeat myself twice before he stopped staring at me and moved.

"I'm mesmerized by your beauty," he told me as he rang up my drinks.

"Not that mesmerized," I told him. "You still charged me ten dollars for two drinks."

I went back to the table and gave my cousin her beer. I sipped the rum and coke. The music playing was from another era so we sat, declining the invitations to dance from the older gentlemen who approached our table what seemed like every three minutes.

Finally a song came on that I liked, Erykah Badu's "Love of my Life." I got up and danced by myself. I came off the dance floor and told my cousin, who seemed to be thoroughly enjoying herself with the other teachers, that I was going to the ladies' room. She waved me on with a smile.

As I walked through the crowd, I saw a group of young guys by the bar. One was sitting on a stool. The others were standing around him. "Finally," I thought, "some guys my age."

As if on some silent cue, the entire group turned to look at me as I walked towards the bar. They looked surprised to see someone their own age as well. I felt nervous, but men, like dogs, can smell fear and I knew that I had to walk with confidence.

As I got closer, the guys standing around the seated guy receded. It was almost mystical. They didn't move physically, just seemed to fade into the background. The room got quieter and time downshifted into slow motion.

I found myself looking into this semi-circle of male figures but all I could see was the guy on the stool in the center. He was looking at me, too. He smiled as I got closer and spoke. "What's your name?"

I had to decide, quickly, whether to give him my real name or an alias. Using an alias is one of my standard dodges when approached by a man. For a reason I could not articulate, I decided on the truth. "Angela."

"I'm Jersey," he told me. "Can I talk to you for a minute?" He exhaled cigarette smoke in my direction as he finished his sentence.

"A minute may be all the time I have," I told him. "You just met me and already you're trying to kill me with second-hand smoke."

He grinned but stubbed his cigarette out. We made small talk and laughed about different people in the room. He tried to get me to dance, but I didn't like any of the songs.

He finally shrugged, got up and danced with three heavy set girls. He made eye contact with me the majority of the time that he was dancing with them. When the song finished, he came back over and plopped down on the stool.

"You just cheated on me with three big girls," I teased him.

"Those girls?" he said pointing back toward them. They waved at him.

"Those," I confirmed.

"Oh, those are my body guards. They got my back." He said it with a straight face. "They know kung fu and sh**."

I stared at him trying to figure out a way to call his bluff but he collapsed into laughter first.

"You're a bad liar," I told him, but I was laughing, too. We talked a little until *I'm Sorry Ms. Jackson* came piping through the speakers. I jumped up and pulled him towards the dance floor. "We can dance to this," I said enthusiastically.

We danced for about three songs. He was light on his feet but it was muggy on the dance floor, so we went to sit down. I casually took him in with my eyes. He was wearing a New York Yankees baseball cap, but I could see a few black curls peeking out on the sides. He looked well put together and had the swagger of a bad boy that attracted me.

"What are you drinking?" he asked over the music.

"Rum and coke," I told him, but then I saw a guy coming towards us selling flowers. "But I'd rather have a rose."

He looked at me if I was crazy. "I'll buy you a drink but not a rose."

"That would be a waste of money because I don't want another drink. I want a rose." I thought the rose would be a nice gesture, a flower isn't a diamond after all, but he saw the rose as a symbol of love and was not going there.

He bought me the drink, but I didn't touch it.

"You're not drinking your drink?" he asked as though he didn't already know the answer to that question.

"I told you I didn't want it. I wanted the rose," I replied.

He frowned, "I am not buying you a rose."

The club lights flashed for last call. I told him that I had to find my cousin and walked away. She was still with the group from the school finishing up their last drinks and conversations. I helped my cousin into her coat and we made our way toward the exit. Halfway there I felt a tap on my shoulder. I turned and there was Jersey.

"Can I get your number?" he asked me with a grin on his face.

I considered him for a minute. I remembered the rose and told him that I didn't give out my number.

He laughed, "Then take my number and you can call me."

"No paper," I told him.

My cousin, always ready to play matchmaker, turned around to get a napkin off the bar but before she could Jersey ripped off a shred of his undershirt. He wrote his number on it and then held it out to me.

I looked at the torn piece of fabric. Then I looked back at his face. "I am not," I told him, "in the habit of accepting phone numbers from strange men."

"What makes you think I'm strange?" he asked me.

"The fact that you are handing me your underwear and not a rose," I told him.

He looked from the shred of white cloth back to me, "This was one of my favorite undershirts. No, it was my very favorite undershirt, and I offer it to you as a souvenir of tonight."

I looked at him and had to smile. "I'm not getting rid of you am I?'

He just grinned. I wrote his number on the napkin my cousin handed me. He walked us to the car. As I unlocked the door, he reached for the handle and held the door open as I got in. "Call me and let me know that you made it home safely," he said in true gentleman fashion.

It might have been a line. He might have used it a dozen times before, but he said it with such sincerity. I couldn't remember any guy I'd met for the first time who had shown the same consideration. I told him I would call and left him standing in the parking lot. In the rear view mirror, I saw him wave to me as we pulled away.

"We must accept life for what it actually is - a challenge to our quality without which we should never know of what stuff we are made, or grow to our full stature."

-*Robert Louis Stevenson*

CHAPTER FOUR

Ready to be Challenged

I got ready for sleep and then sat on the side of the bed, phone in hand, wondering if I should call him. I was so used to the come-on lines guys used that any real statement of consideration rang false to me. "Call me to let me know you got home safe" actually sounded weird. What if this guy were a stalker or dangerous in other ways? My mind reviewed scenes from movies where the nice, innocent guy turned out to be the serial killer.

But I couldn't get his smile and his eyes out of my head. I dialed his number, however, I pushed *67 to block my phone number from showing on his caller ID just in case.

Two rings and I got a message stating that the phone number I had dialed didn't receive calls from blocked numbers. I took a deep breath and called him without blocking.

"Hello," he answered.

"Your bodyguards there or can we talk?" I asked him.

He seemed happy and surprised to hear from me. "I didn't think you were going to call."

"Well, I wanted you to know that I did make it home safely," I told him. "And I wanted to make sure that those three large women hadn't kidnapped you."

And that started our first real conversation. He told me how he loved dogs especially pit bulls. The last girl he dated didn't like the fact that he gave his dog more attention than her. He was Christian but he liked to read about other religions because who was to say that one religion was more right than the other religion. He told me his real name, Dion.

We were on the phone for two hours. I was drifting off to sleep as we said goodnight saying that we would see each other the next day.

I was glad that I had put aside my concerns and called him. I was intrigued and I wanted to know more. For the next month and a half or so we were inseparable.

Even so, the relationship with my journals was still more intimate and in depth than my communications with Dion. I was afraid to let anyone get too close for fear he, or any man, might hurt me. My cardinal rule was to avoid heartbreak. I would have no sympathy for myself if I allowed a man to hurt me. It would be my fault because I allowed myself to love. Still I was lonely, and late one night I wrote a prayer, asking God to send me a man who would challenge me.

Journal Entry

I am ready to be challenged by a man who's ready to meet the champion. I'm the champion of my life, my spirit, my love, my heart, my mind, and my soul. I want to find myself in a sea of your infinite strength. I want to swim in your pool of wisdom. I want you to float in the waters of me, all of me. Dive into me and search for your own soul. That's how deep the waters flow. So deep that you find yourself in me. You find that life, that spirit, that love, that heart, that mind, and that soul. I've been waiting so long for this dance. This chance to get to know who I am when I'm with you.

CHAPTER FIVE

God's Trying to Tell Me Something

Dion lived about ten minutes away from my apartment. Usually I would go to his place after work. We would rent movies or go out to eat. We just had a really good time together. He introduced me to his dog, Joker, a tan pit bull. Joker and I got along. If we were lying in bed watching television, Dion would have one arm around me and the other arm around Joker.

However, I was still not taking off my mask. He seemed like a nice guy...yet, he was still a guy. My cousin teased me about falling in love, but I still had the 'no trespassing' sign up in my heart's front yard. We could have fun, and that's all it had to be.

The distance kept me safe. Protecting my pride was more important to me than finding out what love was all about, but at the same time, I felt alone. Was I not born to love and be loved? I questioned sadness as well as happiness. I wanted answers but I was not sure that I was really ready for them.

What denotes a happy marriage or couple? A big house? Children? Love? I have seen many people who from the outside seem to have it all, but the inner core of the relationship is shaky, and so it ends in divorce. Did they really try to work things out? How long had they felt that way? There were so many questions that I was not sure I really wanted the answers to.

So instead of wanting to create my own fairy tale I just watched my chick flicks and my Disney movies and that could be my love affair. Better to be Julia Roberts in "The Runaway Bride" or Nia Long in "Love Jones" than risk the real pain that was always a part of passion.

And then everything changed.

It wasn't an unusual day. I was on my way to visit Dion driving along South Cobb Drive. The sun was overhead as it should have been. The sky was a normal blue. I was singing along with the radio and then I heard a voice. "I put him in your life for a reason." It seemed to come from both inside and outside of me. I was startled. I'd been thinking about Dion but absent-mindedly, not praying for guidance.

"God is that you?" I actually asked the question out loud. "Dion is in my life for a reason? He has a deeper purpose than just someone to kick it with?" I asked with confusion.

The voice didn't speak again. It didn't have to. The words were still resonating inside me, echoing with a power that seemed to be planting some truth within me.

"What purpose?" I wondered. I reviewed the facts. I'd met Dion at a club. We enjoyed each other. That was it. How could Dion be the one? Where were the fireworks? Why didn't I hear violins playing. And there was one other large looming question.

"How could he be the one," I asked myself, "if I am not even sure that I ever want to get married?"

These questions stayed with me all the way to Dion's front door. I tried to shake the fact that I had been given this revelation. I didn't want to look confused when I saw Dion, mainly because I didn't want to attempt an explanation of the last fifteen minute conversation with God.

Dion opened the door wearing yesterday's clothes and a smile. He kissed me on the cheek and walked back inside, tugging his pants back up to near waist level as he went. He was not like any prince in any book or movie I had ever seen.

"Was he the one? Really?" I didn't know. Who could know? Who ever knows? Even after forty years, I would bet that some questions still linger. But what I was sure of was that a greater wisdom than my own had spoken to me. The voice had been real. I'm not inclined to hallucinations or visions. I don't hear voices. And yet I had.

That night before falling asleep I pulled out my journal and thought about the phenomenon. So now God was telling me that this man was in my life for a reason. Wasn't each person that I came across in my life there to serve a purpose for me at that given moment? What greater purpose did Dion have than the people prior to him or the one's that might come after him?

Journal Entry

As I was driving today on my way to see Dion, I was hit with the thought, well it was more so a revelation, "I put him in your life for a reason." What did God think that by allowing this feeling to come over me was going to happen? I guess God knows that it does not take much for Angela to dismiss guys so I might need to inform her that this one is meant for a deeper purpose, not to be tossed aside if/when he hurts your feelings or simply says something that you don't like. If this is true God, please help me to find this purpose quickly.

"There are no greater treasures than the highest human qualities such as compassion, courage and hope. Not even tragic accident or disaster can destroy such treasures of the heart."

-Daisaku Ikeda

CHAPTER SIX

Crash

My birthday was in February and my mom was coming to visit. I hadn't told her about Dion yet, because I wasn't sure what to tell her. When she got into town we went shopping and then out to eat. Over lunch, she asked the usual questions, wanting to know about my friends and if there were anyone special around. I told her that I had a friend but that he was nothing more than a friend.

Later that night I had a date with some friends for dinner. My mom let me take her C230 Mercedes Benz. I swung by to visit Dion. When he answered the door, I swept my arm out toward the parked Mercedes, "My birthday present from my mom," I told him proudly.

His jaw about dropped to the floor. He looked from the car to me and back again and that was as long as I could keep a straight face. I had to admit that I was kidding.

He looked at me up and down and told me that I was looking good. "If I was your man," he told me, "I don't think I could handle you going out like that without me by your side."

I looked him in the eye. "So you think you can handle being my man?"

Without blinking or hesitating, he said, "I can handle it."

A couple of days later he gave me a birthday card which he signed 'Love Dion'. I didn't read much into it. I just figured that he couldn't think of any other salutation so he wrote 'Love'.

Later that week his next door neighbor invited us over for dinner. Dion and I were in the kitchen fixing our plates when Dion began to tickle me. The man came in the kitchen to find out what all the commotion was. He saw us playing and said, "I believe she is the only thing that will ever get between you and your dog."

Emotions continued to escalate. He was so easy to be with. Without making a conscious choice, I found myself letting my mask slip, if only just a little. I started thinking of Dion as my man.

A week later, we went to his mother's house to visit his brother and sister-in-law, Tommy and Jess. A couple of cousins were there along with some other friends. Everyone seemed pretty cool. The girls watched the guys play pool until the guys went outside to smoke. The girls stayed in the house sitting around talking. This was not my idea of the perfect evening. A little family time was okay but I had hoped we would leave early and be alone together. A couple of hours drug by and we finally got up to go. As we were leaving he asked me to drive his truck because he had too much to drink.

We didn't speak the whole ride. I was so ready to get back to his house so that I could get in my car and go back to my apartment. I pulled his truck into the driveway next to my car. We got out and as I was walking around to get into my car he stopped me. "What's wrong?"

"Nothing." At least nothing I was willing to name.

Of course he didn't believe me, so he asked again, "Angela, what is wrong?"

I told him that I was fine. He still pushed for more. I finally told him that I had wanted to spend my evening with him and not his family. It was cool to meet them but I didn't think we were going to be over there all night. "I wanted to spend more time with you alone." This was a big admission for me…to admit needing something, anything, from a man.

"So you're mad because we didn't have any time alone… just the two of us?" he asked.

"A little."

"We could be alone now. Come on in and stay the night."

It seemed to be an easy answer but I was feeling exposed and uneasy. I just wanted to retreat to my place. We kissed each other goodnight and then I got in my car. I shifted into reverse and started backing out looking into the rearview mirror. I never saw the front end of my car swing around to smack the back bumper of Dion's truck. I felt the impact and heard the crush of metal. I slammed on the brakes and sat there in shock with the back end of my car in the middle of the street.

Dion came around to the front of my car to survey the damage. "Pull back," he called to me. I did, but hesitated at the sound of shrieking metal. "Keep going." I did and finally the two vehicles broke clear of each other with a shudder.

I was so embarrassed. I just knew he was going to kill me. Guys love their cars. I got out to inspect the damage. The side of my car over the left front tire was smashed in. I timidly walked over to him. He had climbed into his truck and had his head down.

"Dion?" I called to him.

He looked up at me. I knew he was going to curse me out. I was ready for it. Heck, I deserved it, but what came out of his mouth surprised me. "Are you okay?" he asked with great concern.

"Uh, yeah," I stuttered. "I'm fine." But I was stunned and confused. I didn't know how to respond. I had just made a fool of myself, trashed his truck and he was concerned about my well-being. No cursing, no rampage, no look what you did to my ride, just, "Are you okay?"

"It's not too bad," he told me. "We can work it out with the insurance in the morning." He asked me again to stay the night but I was too ashamed. He looked worried. "Call me to let me know you made it home safely."

At home, I sat on the side of the bed in disbelief about what had just happened. I called him. He was still asking me if I was okay. I told him that I would be. I told him that I would pay for any damages. He told me not to worry about it

The next morning driving to work, the tire scraped against the inside of the wheel well with every rotation. The worst of this was that I was covered by my parent's insurance and would have to tell them. I rehearsed how the conversation would go.

"Hi. It's me Angela. I got some good news and bad news. I'm okay but last night, my boyfriend was too drunk to drive so I drove his truck home, parked it in his driveway and then got into my own car, shifted the transmission into reverse and slammed backwards into the truck I had just parked thirty seconds earlier. Hello? Mom? Dad?"

They wouldn't be worried about the damage or insurance. They would be very interested in the news that I had a boyfriend, and one that drank to excess would just be icing on the cake.

I didn't want to lie to them but I didn't think that I really needed to tell them the whole truth. I ended up telling them that I hit a friend's car and he wasn't going to charge me to fix his car.

The car wreck accelerated the emotional charge between us which also felt like it was heading for some kind of a collision. The next week, Dion wanted to watch the movie Brown Sugar. I loved that movie, so I had no problem.

I put the disc in the player and snuggled down on the bed beside him. As the opening credits rolled, he pulled me closer to him. I eventually ended up with my head on his chest and my ear against his heart. I could hear his heart beating.

I was actively engaged in the movie as if I had never seen it before. I felt like Dion wasn't as interested. I turned to him, slightly lifting my head off of his chest. "You okay?" I asked looking up into his eyes.

"Fine," he said. So I turned back around to continue watching the movie.

He was stroking my hair and I felt his heart beat speed up a bit. "I love you," he said in a scared, gentle voice. In my head, I saw Dion and I on a roller coaster. We were in the lead car sitting side by side. The car was just about to crest the top of the steepest climb and then go hurtling down into some kind of unknown oblivion.

I knew I had to choose my words carefully. I thought a minute and then said, "Huh?"

"Did you hear me?" he asked. "I said 'I love you.'"

He looked at me with this intensity, this burning question and I knew what his question was - was I going to say 'I love you' back.

I had to say something. I couldn't leave him there with his heart out in the open. I didn't feel that I was in love at that point and I didn't want to lead him on so I decided on the truth. I opened my mouth and out came, "I love you too." I clapped my hand over my mouth as if I could keep the words already loose in the world from escaping.

Dion's faced lit up like the sun. Any chance of taking back my words was gone.

I gave him a kiss and turned back to watch the movie, which now held no interest for me. In my own head, I was rationalizing my response. If this was not love that I was feeling now, who was to say that I would not love him in the future. I remembered God's voice telling me that Dion was the one.

What made this even stranger was that I was falling in love with a guy who came from a different world than me. He didn't just have a bad boy's swagger, he had a bad boy's lifestyle. A lot of his friends made me nervous.

Dion came from a family like mine. His mother was an international consultant and his Dad a chiropractor. They divorced when he was four but he seemed to handle it okay. He was a happy kid who did well in school until he was nine years old.

He moved that summer to live with his father and his family. Dion had a cousin who was seven or eight years older. This cousin was a real bad boy with several arrests and convictions. As any young boy might, Dion looked up to his cousin and sometimes copied his behavior. In time, this tough guy, bad boy persona became Dion's own mask. He would put it on to protect himself or to project himself. Like a superhero's costume, Dion's mask helped him to take on the world and the forces that he felt opposed him. The problem was that he could take it too far sometimes and did have a few run-ins with the police. He had even spent a few days in jail.

That night I fell asleep in his arms. I drifted off comforted by the fact that he loved me. Somehow he hadn't allowed the invisible wall I had built around my heart to keep him from wanting to love me. Little by little, he'd broken down my old way of thinking. He got me to want to be in love with love rather than just the concept of love. The next morning I went to work confident in the fact that I was loved and no one could take that away from me.

Journal Entry

Through experience after experience I came into my own understanding of love. I realized that as a child I was in love with the concept of love. As a woman I wanted love to be some type of fairy tale romantic comedy because the real life love was just too confusing. I yearned for a kiss that would always be there when I awakened in the morning...The high that waited for me when I got home and the feeling of wanting to do it all over again tomorrow. The day he would take my hand tell me that this dream would never end.

Who wants to be loved? I didn't. It was too confusing. It was too complicated. It was too crazy.

Who wants to be loved? I did and I do, because it's so wonderful. It's so amazing. It's so encouraging. Love is confusing yet wonderful.

"Commitment is an act, not a word."

-*Jean Paul Sartre*

CHAPTER SEVEN
Living Arrangements

A week later, our investment in this relationship got a real test. Dion and I were in my car. I could tell something was on his mind. Finally he looked over at me and said, "I have to be out of my house by the end of April. I need to start looking for a place to stay."

I got a dark, heavy feeling in the pit of my stomach knowing where this conversation was going.

He turned to me with a smile, "When's your lease up?"

I told him that my lease was up in June. Before he could say anything else, I said a silent prayer. "Don't let him ask me to move in with him. I just met him. Okay, not just, three months ago but please, it's too soon."

"How would you feel about getting a place together? When your lease is up?"

New thoughts and questions flooded my head, "Oh, no I don't think so. We just met. He could be crazy. He could kill me in my sleep. Hell, my parents would kill me as soon as they found out." Instead of voicing my concerns though, I said, "We might be able to do that."

I knew I should have said "No." I knew that my parents would never approve of me moving in with some guy before we were married. And still I had bailed on my answer. I was disappointed with myself and not completely sure of what was

33

going on in my head. My mother had called me Hard Hearted Hanna for most of my life for the disdainful way I treated my dates and would-be boyfriends. I'd never had a problem delivering the truth and often took pleasure in the power my words could carry. But here I was with Dion acting uncertain and babbling.

I waited a week before I told him that my parents would not allow me to move in with him. I hadn't even talked to my parents about moving in with him. I know I should have told him the truth, but I didn't want him to be upset with me. So I put it off on my parents.

I really was torn. I was afraid that not moving in with Dion might end our relationship and I was also afraid that moving in with Dion could end our relationship. The dilemma was solved the next week when Dion told me that he was about to get a new job working at a warehouse. His shift would be from 3 pm to 3 am. I looked at him in disbelief. I knew that he needed to work but these hours were ridiculous. There would be no time to see each other anymore.

I sighed and said "I guess you're damned if you do and damned if you don't." He needed to spend time making money which for now was going to take priority over our spending time together. What could I say?

That weekend I had to go home to celebrate my father's birthday. I told Dion I would call him when I got back to town and we could continue our discussion.

It was a good weekend, but I missed Dion. I couldn't wait to see him when I got back to Atlanta. I called him as soon as I unpacked. He didn't answer. I waited a few minutes and called him again. This time he answered but sounded tired. I told him that I'd made it back into town. He didn't seem too excited by the news. We were on the phone maybe two minutes when he told me that he needed to call me back.

I waited about forty-five minutes for him to call. Nothing. I called him, no answer. I waited about another hour or so. Dion still didn't call. The next day was Monday. I had to go to work and I was tired from the trip so I got ready for bed.

I called him again as I was sliding under the covers. He still didn't answer. I wondered if he was mad at me. What was going on? I finally went to sleep, but it wasn't a sound sleep. I kept having the same dream over and over. We were in a roller coaster, Dion and me in the front car, rolling over the crest of the steepest drop and then hurtling downwards. I could see, between the fingers of my hands covering my face as I screamed, that the tracks ended in mid-air about twenty yards ahead of us. In each successive dream, as our car got to the end of the tracks, just before sailing off into a lightless void, I would wake up, not screaming but sweating and gasping for air.

I was tired and worried at school the next day, but I taught the children as I always did. I couldn't allow them to see me looking distracted. This struggle went on Tuesday as well because I didn't hear from Dion until Wednesday afternoon.

He called to say that he was coming over later. By the time later came, I was getting ready to go to bed. He apologized for not calling me and blamed it on his new job and being tired.

He told me that he had moved, but he didn't have his phone set up yet. I was happy to see him, but I wasn't sure if I could deal with his new hours and their impact on our time together. The thought also occurred to me that he may not be telling me the whole truth.

That night we slept cradled together. He would not have it any other way. The next morning, I walked him to the door and gave him a hug and kiss. I watched him walk away down the hall. He turned at the corner before the stairwell and looking back, he gave me a wave and a half smile.

That smile stalled the world into slow motion. It felt like the first night I had met him. Like a scene from a movie, one person walking away, turning their head back with a sad smile. The other person, me, just standing there while the world receded from them.

As Dion walked away, I had this feeling that this would be the last time I would see him. I tried to shake the feeling but deep down I felt that it was true. Our roller coaster car had jumped the tracks and I was falling into the unknown.

CHAPTER EIGHT

Time to Process

For the next few months, I had no way to contact Dion. He would call me and leave messages but always on my land line phone during the hours I was at work. He never called my cell phone which made me believe that he didn't really want to talk to me. He just wanted me to know that he was thinking of me.

I was never big on crying for any reason. And I definitely didn't believe in crying over a guy. This time was different. I don't know why, I just cried. I wanted to hate him for hurting me but I couldn't. The more time that passed, the more I found myself loving him.

I was furious with myself. This was exactly why I had not allowed myself to love before. I wanted to avoid the hurt of not knowing what went wrong. I hated sitting alone, questioning the silence. I knew I was right to protect myself against the pain. He was not there, shouldn't I hate him? What was going on? Where was he? Was he okay? "God, please protect him and keep him safe. I love him," I prayed daily.

Journal Entry

Lord, why am I longing for love in the noisy silence of my mind. Do I really want now, what I keep denying I wanted ever? Am I on a search to find my friend or is he looking for me? How did I meet him? Have I lost him? Are there any men out there on a search to find a good thing and a good thing only. Am I made to be loved unconditionally by a man or

*have I blown my chance? Falling in love is easy, but
getting, back up is not. I've had lovers and crushes
and I want one true love...one for me.*

Prior to Dion, if a guy left me, I would think of all the
things that I didn't like about him. I'd transform him into an
inconsiderate jerk and then not care what happened to him. This
time it was different? I was different. I loved him, without
question and instead of thinking bad thoughts or talking badly
about him, I decided to do what had seen me through other hard
times. I prayed for him. I prayed that he was safe and out of
danger's way. I prayed that somehow he knew that I wasn't mad
at him and that I was actually sending love his way. I didn't pray
that we'd see each other again but I did have that hope in my
heart.

The spring passed with me in a love sick haze. The school
year ended in May. I knew that I wasn't going to renew my
contract with that daycare facility so I decided to move back
home to Nashville. I didn't want to be at home but I had no
other choice. Once there, I was at such a loss for what to do
with my time that I started going to Bible Study at my church.

The teacher, Dr. Jackson, asked me what I wanted to do
with my life. I told him that I was ready to go back to school to
get my master's degree, however, I didn't know what I wanted to
study. I did know it had to be something in education, because
I come from a long line of teachers, principals, and librarians.
Some kind of educator DNA pumps in my veins.

Dr. Jackson gave me a spiritual gifts inventory to do which
consisted of about fifty questions, an answer key, and a bar
graph. When he scored my answers the results pointed to
counseling. I'd never considered counseling as a profession. I
found this very interesting. I went online to search for colleges
with programs in counseling and guidance that were in cities that
I might like to call home.

The first college that Google served up was New York University. New York City was an exciting place to live and what better place to learn about counseling diverse populations than in a city of extreme and wonderful diversity. I printed out an application.

I also looked at a few other places, however, New York University had my attention. My application had to be mailed by February 2, 2004, which I found to be a good sign because that was also my birthday!

I started the process of getting my transcript from Clark Atlanta University and letters of recommendation. I wrote in my journal "I will be in someone's counseling and guidance program in the fall of 2004."

No longer was I concerned with being in love with Dion. I figured he would find me when it was the right time. I focused on finding a deeper meaning and purpose for myself. What was I supposed to do in this lifetime? What was my contribution to the world? Instead of dreaming about a love to sweep me off my feet, I started to find out what my passion for life was. What was I good at that I could do for a living that could potentially make a difference in this world?

Journal Entry

Lord, I feel the call for my heart to become a change agent. I truly want to be a blessing to all I come in contact with, children and adults. I get along with a variety of people and that is a blessing in and of itself. I want to make a difference in the lives of many. I need your help and strength and patience.

I completed gathering all the materials for my application and sent them off to New York. I was nervous, really wanting to be accepted. I'd been so focused on this new path that I had almost forgotten about Dion and then, riding home from a restaurant with my brother, I got a phone call. I looked at my watch. It was past 12 am. The caller ID on my cell showed a 770 area code. I figured I must know this person if they were bold enough to call me this late. I answered the phone and a familiar voice said, "Hello, it's me Jersey."

I jerked the phone away from ear. Could this be? I wanted to make sure I had heard him right. "Who?"

"Dion." He sounded defeated already, as if he expected me to curse him out at his audacity to call me after such a long time. The truth was I didn't know what to do. Part of me wanted to curse him out and another part wished I could hug him right through the phone. I spoke to him for a minute or so and then asked if I could call him back when I got home. He said that I would be able to reach him at the number that he called from. I could tell that he didn't believe that I was going to call him back.

I didn't want to talk to him while I was riding with my brother because I think it is rude to carry on a long conversation with someone else and not talk to the person you're with. Also, I needed sometime to process the avalanche of thoughts and feelings his call had set off.

When I got home I got ready for bed and looked at the number on my cell phone. It was hard to believe he had called. I called him back thinking, hoping he would answer.

He sounded surprised, "Hi. I didn't think that you were going to call me back. I figured that you were mad at me."

"I am. It's been ten months."

"I don't blame you." There was a short silence and then a conversation began that lasted for three hours. He told me that he had not been able to find an apartment on his own and had moved in with his ex-girlfriend. He said that if we had moved in together he would have proposed to me within three months. He told me how sorry he was and how he prayed for me every night. He told me that he loved me and that he prayed if God ever gave him another chance that he would do right by me.

I accepted his apologies. I thought about a song that came out that summer of 2003 by Jagged Edge, *Walked Outta Heaven*. The chorus kept playing in my mind:

> *Feels like I just walked right out of heaven*
> *Feels like I have damn near thrown my life away,*
> *Hey, yea yea*
> *Scared, just like a child that's lost at seven*
> *Don't know what to do, gotta get right with you*
> *Feels like I just walked right out of heaven.*

Every time I'd heard the song, I'd hoped that he was listening at the same time and was feeling bad about leaving me without saying goodbye.

And then, without me asking, he told me that he felt like the Jagged Edge song. He said that the song described the way he felt. He kept apologizing to me. I wanted him to feel bad for what he had done, but by this point I knew he was sorry. It seemed that my wishing and hoping and praying had worked. He cried on the phone that night.

I told him that the entire time I was away from him I had been praying for his safety and well-being. I felt like I should have been crying right along with him, but I couldn't. I was too happy and surprised that I was even speaking to him again.

He wanted me to take him back that night. "How will I know that you won't do this again?" I asked.

"I won't. I learned my lesson."

The fact was no matter what he said, no matter how much he assured me that he wouldn't leave me again, there was always a possibility that he would. I told him that I wasn't sure if I could really do this.

He told me he understood. When I hung up the phone, it took me a while to settle down. The last thing I heard before falling asleep was the echo of the voice, "He's in your life for a purpose."

Talk about if you let something go that you love if it is meant to be it will come back to you. I had let go of ever hearing from him again. However, I had not let go of the hope. I had allowed myself to love a man. And then I was hurt by that man. And then I surprised myself by not hating him but by sending love to him through my prayers. And then he came back to me full of apology. And now I had to figure out if I was going to allow myself to risk loving again.

Journal Entry

Wow! I do not know what to say. It was him! There was Jersey! I knew I didn't hate him but I didn't know just exactly how fond the heart grows in such absence. He told me how much he loved me and that he wanted to prove it to me. He said he was sorry for hurting me and that he would never do anything to hurt me again.

I love him. No, I do. I can't explain why but we went through more stuff in two months the most couples came through in a lifetime. Those things made me a little stronger and made him want to be a better person. I don't know why I love him but I'm so glad that he is safe and not wanting to be a part of what he was.

*I pray that you allow me to see him again, hold him
again, and kiss him again. Lord, help me to figure out
exactly what you want to come of this relationship.*

Some last minute business related to my application to
NYU sent me back to Atlanta that next week. I had to interview
one of my Clark professors face to face to make sure that he
would send my recommendation letter on time. I might have
been able to pull it off over the phone but this also gave me a
chance to see Dion. On the drive to Atlanta, I was nervous and
excited. I told myself to take things slowly but my heart was
racing by the time I pulled up to his house. He was outside
waiting for me. We awkwardly hugged then he helped me with
my bags.

We walked inside and then we looked at each other. All the
emotion of the past months welled up, for both of us. We
grabbed each other in a hug that lasted for minutes. Then he
pulled back a little, looking into my face. Slowly, he leaned down
and kissed me. I had not realized how much I had missed his
kisses.

"There is a price to pay for accomplishment."

-Edwin Louis Cole

CHAPTER NINE
Acceptance

I never talked to my mom, or really any of my family members, about guys in my life. I've always kept that part of my life to myself but one day my mother and I were driving and I decided to open up to her about Dion. I figured that I needed all the advice I could get.

I told her about us being together when I was living in Atlanta. I also told her that he had left me without so much as a goodbye but now he was back in my life and he wanted me to be his girlfriend again.

She didn't think that it was a good idea for me to take him back, "How do you know he won't do it again?" She asked.

"I don't," I responded. "But I am willing to see what will happen."

We went back and forth, at times angrily, until we arrived back home. My mother stopped to retrieve our mail. She was in mid-sentence about how a horse cannot change its spots when she handed me a big white envelope. The logo for New York University was in the upper left hand corner.

I imagined that I had overlooked something in my original application and this was a request for more documentation. I opened the envelope and started to read. "Congratulations you have been accepted into Steinhardt School of Education for Counseling and Guidance K-12."

I read it three more times before erupting, "Oh my gosh, I got accepted to New York University." I couldn't believe it, they actually wanted me. "WOW! Momma I got accepted to New York University!"

She erupted right along with me. "We are going to New York!" She was ready to shop. I was still in shock.

I couldn't wait to inform Dion of my good news. I called him up. "D, I got accepted to New York University!"

"Congratulations baby, I am so proud of you."

I heard him saying congratulations, however, I was not sure that he really happy for me? "What will this mean for us, Dion?" I asked him. "We're already separated, but New York to Georgia is even further. "

His response left me with my mouth and heart open. "We will make it work. I can't risk losing you again."

What could I say but, "Okay." I was still on the fence about trusting him again but he seemed willing to wait for me to climb over the railing and back into his arms.

About a month or so later he did admit to me that he was actually sad about my moving to New York, but he didn't want to tell me because he didn't want to get me down. He didn't like that we were far away from each other, but he wanted me to pursue my dreams.

And that little bit of honesty, opened my heart again. My feelings found their way onto my journal pages that night.

Journal Entry

I write tonight to tell you I love you. I thought maybe it is not love but lust or maybe even infatuation. But it didn't really hit me until the distance made me realize that I could not do without you. I love you!

From the beginning of the relationship something told me that we were meant to teach each other a lesson. It was not until now that I realized that the lesson was: don't be afraid to love. Dion, you taught me patience and you made me want to love you even though I didn't think I was ready to love. I hope I taught you that love will not turn its back on you even when you turn your back on love. Love should grow and mature and learn from your mistakes. Love cries. Love smiles. Love sings. Love laughs. I love you now and I loved you then.

My mother, father and brother drove me to New York City. We were going to stay with my cousin in Brooklyn, but my father didn't feel comfortable leaving the van full of my belongings parked on the street. We decided to stay at the hotel about ten minutes away.

The next day we drove to the dorms known as Stuy Town on 20th St and 1st Ave. Stuy Town was an apartment building. The owners allowed NYU to use some of the apartments as housing for students. My cousin Bonita and her fiancé helped us move all my stuff in a single day. We had dinner and then my parents and brother got back on the road to Tennessee.

I met my roommate, Layla, the next day. She was from California and here to study for a Masters in Social Work. Anytime something was bothering her she didn't hesitate to talk to me about it and I did the same with her. I loved living with a fellow mental health student. It was like getting free therapy!

Most of our sessions were over some kind of chocolate! I made a lot of friends in the counseling field. I also met Joanna who lived down the hall. She was also in a long distance relationship. We spent the first hour talking about our boyfriends. She told me that if we were to break up it would not be because of the distance. This was an 'aha' moment for me. Distance would be the excuse but there were always underlying factors that must be taken into account.

Dion called me every day and every night. Whenever I had a late class, he wanted me to call him to let him know that I made it back to my apartment safely. I liked his support which really came through in a big way on my cancer walk.

Prior to going to New York, I made a commitment to walk for the Avon Breast Cancer Walk the first weekend in October, twenty-six miles around New York City. I didn't know anyone that was willing to do the walk with me, so I did it by myself.

I walked with women who were breast cancer survivors and women who were walking for their mothers, sisters, aunts, friends. There were even a few men walking. What touched me the most were the women walking who were still going through chemotherapy. These women were already tired from battling with cancer and now they were out here walking for the cure. A few times I had to stop myself from tearing up.

The first day we did a little over thirteen miles. We had dinner and went to sleep in tents under the Williamsburg Bridge. Even though I was tucked into my sleeping bag, I was still cold. Alone in a big tent with sore ankles and feet, I tossed and turned most of the night wondering what had I gotten myself into.

I called Dion. "Dion, I do not think I can continue the walk tomorrow."

"Why not baby?"

"My feet and ankles hurt. I don't think I trained enough. I am so tired." I had a lot of complaints.

Dion became my cheerleader. "You didn't go up there to walk thirteen miles and quit did you?"

"No, but I didn't think that walking would be this hard. My feet hurt."

"You knew how far you were walking when you signed up and now you want to back out?"

"I am not backing out. Some people stopped earlier today."

"I think if you did thirteen miles today, then you can do thirteen miles tomorrow. There are things worse than sore feet. That's why you're there. Right?"

I wasn't explaining myself very well. I wanted him to feel my pain or at least feel sorry for me. He told me that I could do it and that he was proud of me. We got off the phone saying, 'I love you'.

I appreciated his not giving in to my whining and complaining. I needed him to be that way with me. I knew better than to give up. After all I wasn't walking for myself.

The next morning I noticed a tent that I hadn't seen yesterday. Inside the tent women were giving foot massages. I went in and a woman with magic hands undid the knots in my feet. I almost bounced out of the tent, got a little bite to eat, grabbed a water and I was back to walking for a cure. At the end of the last 13.3 miles I arrived at the finish line. There was a sea of pink shirts crossing the Brooklyn Bridge. Women were walking arm in arm and hugging their loved ones as they reached the finish line. I didn't have anyone to walk arm in arm with or to hug, yet I was still proud of myself. I allowed one tear to drop.

That weekend was a kind of baptism into being a New Yorker. I mingled with a lot of strangers and found out I was tougher than I thought. But each day that fall as I walked down the sidewalks, I couldn't quite believe I was in New York City. I'd always thought moving there would be scary, but it wasn't. I was here working on my master's degree. For a girl that never cared for school to now be in graduate school at a prestigious university suggested that anything just might be possible. Dion says that we can do this distance thing, so I'm willing to believe that we can.

Journal Entry

I'm in New York now and have been here for a week and five days. Country girl moves to the big city. I love my mom, dad and brother but I don't miss them like most people would expect that I would. There's someone else in my life that I didn't realize I would miss so much. Nor did I think that my love for him would get stronger with this distance. Each day I love him as if love were going out of style. I've never felt this way about anyone before in my life and I don't believe I will be able to feel this way again nor do I believe I should have to. Even though I feel that he is all wrong for me his love feels so right our love has never felt stronger and yet we are so far apart. Last week we got into a disagreement about money. I heard his side; he heard my side and we moved on. We're basically miserable because we can't see each other. He told me he cried for me. He can be a real sweetheart.

CHAPTER TEN

Do You Trust Me?

I went to visit Dion in Atlanta the second weekend in October. He picked me up from the airport and took me to our favorite pizza place, Fellini's. He wanted to sit outside. I didn't understand why because it was cold but he gave me his coat so that I would be warmer.

Once we got outside, I realized that we were sitting at the same table that we had sat at before. It was his way of being romantic. He was building special places and memories for us. He'd bought me roses and a card. Inside the card was a poem that he'd written for me.

> *When I think of you my heart jumps.*
> *My body gets a cold chill and then immediately gets warm.*
> *The thought of you makes me smile.*
> *The love you give is unforgettable.*
> *The way you walk is hypnotizing.*
> *The way you speak is soothing.*
> *The way you feel is heavenly.*
> *The way you kiss is healing.*
> *The way you taste is addicting.*
> *The way you sleep is precious.*
> *The way you look at me is priceless.*
> *But of all the ways you make me feel*
> *the way you love me is the best feeling of all.*

He also wrote on the card: The girl of my dreams I met on January 11, 2003. My girl is a beautiful person inside and out. She is a caring and loving person. She is also my best friend. She is very smart. She is strong. She is always on my mind. She is the best thing that ever happened to me. She is my love.

We made the most of our time together that weekend. We went to the movies and out to eat. The geographic distance between us most days made this time together more intense, more special.

Dion had to go into work that Monday morning, but he was coming back to take me to the airport. While I was getting ready to leave, my old trust issues surfaced. I didn't like leaving him and I couldn't shake the feeling that he was hiding something from me. I looked around in his room. Hidden in a coat pocket I found a note addressed to a female. I knew that I shouldn't have opened it, but I couldn't help myself. Dion didn't write to me, so why was he writing to this other girl. I read it. His words expressed how much he missed this girl and the things they used to do together. I was hurt and confused, and incredibly pissed.

The letter was dated two weeks earlier. Written about the same time he'd asked me to come see him because he missed me so much. Instead of confronting him, I packed my bags and set this letter along with one of my own telling him 'it's over' on the edge of his bed.

I made sure that I was ready to walk out of the door when he came back so that he wouldn't see my note until after I was gone. When he came home though, he squeezed around me at the front door saying that he needed to get something out of his room.

He took me by the hand and pulled me along with him. Amber, his two year old niece, tagged along as well. He didn't notice the letters on the edge of his bed but Amber began to shuffle through the papers. He asked her what she was looking at and then he recognized the letter he had written.

He looked at me in disbelief, "Why were you going through my things?"

I told him that I felt like he was keeping something from me, so I snooped. I was crying and telling him that I didn't trust him and I didn't want to be with him if he still had these feelings for her.

He was mad that I had gone through his things but he was more scared that I would leave him. He apologized over and over again. He told me that it was a just a note to say good-bye. He had left her like he had left me, with no explanation. "I wrote the note because I know now that was wrong to just leave. And I know it was wrong because of you."

I calmed down. A little. Logically, this made some sense to me as I re-read the note in my mind but I needed to get back to New York City so that I could think. On the way to the airport, he asked if we were okay at least twenty times. He called me once as I sat on the plane. He asked me to call him when I got back to New York.

When I arrived back at my apartment I started putting my stuff away and contemplating my relationship with Dion. I was mad. I was scared. I was hurt. And I was still in love. The least I could do was call him, so that he didn't have to worry about my safety. All I wanted to do was let him know that I was back safe.

He asked me how I was doing now that I was back in New York City. "You said that you would not hurt me again." I told him.

"I am sorry, baby."

And then I heard the echo of the voice. "He's in your life for a purpose." The voice was so clear it felt like I was holding two conversations at the same time. I told Dion that I needed a minute. He told me to call him back when I was ready.

As soon as I hung up the phone, I began to pace the parquet floors. I looked up toward the ceiling, actually through the ceiling and I asked God a question, okay several questions. "What am I supposed to do now? You say that he is in my life for a reason, for a bigger purpose, right? So, what purpose is this serving now? I must love him or I would have just let him go; no looking back, like I would do when any other guy made me mad. Tell me what I am supposed to do now God."

At that point my phone rang. I didn't want any interruptions. I wanted God to give me my answer. But what if this were God on the phone? Not actually God, the omnipotent being, but his answer being relayed over the phone line? After the third ring I picked up.

It was Dion. He didn't say hello and he didn't ask me if I was finished thinking about it. He asked me a question that would not generally be posed on the brink of breaking up.

"Angela," I heard him say. "Will you marry me?"

My heart and brain crashed together, "What?"

"Will you marry me?" he said. What was crazy was that he asked it like he was just asking an ordinary question. It was asked no differently than asking where I might want to have dinner.

Then something strange happened over which I seemingly had no control. My mouth opened and out came the word, "YES!" I was either crazy or in love.

It surprised Dion, too. "Are you serious?" he asked.

"Yes, I am serious," I said. In that moment I knew that I loved him more than anything.

He apologized for the letter again and said he just wanted to get some things off his chest about how he was feeling. I said that is all well and good to let your feelings out on paper, but you should have burned it up or thrown it away. He laughed. We talked until both our voices were weighted with exhaustion.

"You should go to sleep." He offered. "You have an early class tomorrow."

"You're probably right." I told him.

"And besides," he almost whispered, "I have to get up early and find you a ring."

I hung up. I was fuzzy but far from sleep. Was this how the princess felt when the prince's kiss wakened her from a lifelong sleep? Happy, but confused, too? She had to be. I was, but I was also ready to lay down my mask, put on his ring, and finally, fully be Angela.

We had to wait two months until New Year's Eve to actually be together again. I drove to Atlanta to his mom's house where he was staying. Joy welcomed me telling me that Dion was just getting out of the shower.

As I waited for him to come down, I noticed really pretty flowers in a vase. I complimented Joy on her flowers.

She smiled at me and said, "Those are your flowers. Dion got them for you."

I looked around again paying attention to the actual variety of flowers, three vibrant pink roses that were surrounded by yellow daisies and pale pink sweetheart roses, baby's breath as well as some orange flowers that I did not recognize. These flowers were no longer "pretty," they were beautiful.

When Dion finally came down stairs I gave him a big hug and waited for him to say something about the flowers. He gave me a Happy New Year card and he told me that the flowers belonged to me.

He then proceeded to show me a diamond catalogue. "I've picked out the ring I want to buy you."

I really could not believe that he had actually picked out the ring already. It was very pretty, but it was too much for me. I am a simple girl and Dion sometimes liked the whole gaudy bling effect.

I knew he was serious about loving me but I was not sure of why he was so ready to marry me. Or maybe it was me that was serious about loving him, but I was not sure about marriage. What had seemed like a good idea with a thousand miles between us felt a little less certain now that we were face to face.

Journal Entry

Whoa! Marriage! Marriage? Me? He? Marriage, huh? I love him, I really do, but marriage. Period. He says he wants to marry me and buy me an engagement ring. I'm ready for love, but marriage? I want a ring but am I ready for a ring. Hell is he a ready for a ring.

I only hope that this is our last argument for a long time. Lord, keep him focused about school and starting his own company. I want him to be prosperous and I know he could be. No matter what happens between us, God, I honestly want you to bless him abundantly.

CHAPTER ELEVEN

Distance From New York to Florida

He'd asked me what I wanted for Christmas and I told him a Build-A-Bear. Once he figured out what a Build-A-Bear was he told me that he wasn't going to get me one. This reminded me of our first meeting when he had declined to buy me a rose. A bear was too much like a rose to him. Too sentimental or sappy.

Instead, he bought me Penelope, the second to the largest pink FAO Schwartz dog. He also got me a little teddy bear holding a heart, and a huge bouquet of flowers. But his biggest surprise was the big news that he had been accepted into Motorcycle Mechanics Institute (MMI) in Orlando, Florida.

I knew that this was a big deal for him, and for us. His plan was to get certified as a motorcycle mechanic and eventually open his own shop. This was his way to turn his passion into his livelihood.

He also told me that he was getting a yellow and black Honda CBR 1000 for Christmas from his parents. I snuck out the next day and bought him a black and yellow backpack. Inside I hid a motorcycle calendar, pens, pencils, paper, and a note of encouragement.

He had to leave for Florida in mid-January. I knew that it would be hard for him to move away from his family, but I also knew that this was the start of building our life together. He wanted me to go to Florida with him to help him move in but I had to get back to New York.

I wasn't able to see Dion again until my Spring Break in March. Three weeks before I was scheduled to go down, he was in a motorcycle accident. His front wheel hit a curb and he was thrown about fifty feet. He said it was as if God put a pillow underneath him when he landed. "I didn't feel anything." He had a few bumps and bruises but nothing more serious. When I got off the phone with him, I cried. I was happy that he hadn't been hurt but I was worried about him. I couldn't wait for the weeks to pass so that I could hold him.

I left New York on a late winter's day and landed in Florida to sunshine and seventy five degrees. The light breeze felt wonderful. I loved being surrounded by palm trees. I stayed with Dion the entire week and we did the simplest but sweetest things.

We talked about a lot of different stuff, family, friends, and past relationships. Out of the blue he said "Angela, you're the best thing that ever happened to me."

I was speechless. "Wow, really, I don't know what to say!" And then I did. "Your love for me is the greatest thing that could have ever happened to me."

The week ended too soon. On the plane ride home, a new thought hit me. I had put down my mask. I was no longer just an actress in my life, I was living it. I was still afraid from time to time but I spent more of my days letting love move me where it would. I wasn't hiding. I looked at my reflection in the plane's window. I looked the same on the outside, but the mask was gone.

CHAPTER TWELVE

Questioning Peace

That summer and most of the fall flew by in a haze of activity. We saw each other more. We fought less, but we still had our moments, some of which were around our living arrangements. Our school programs in Florida and at NYU would keep us living in separate cities at least until May of 2006 when I graduated. Dion's mechanic courses would last another year and on a regular basis, he asked me if I would come to Florida to live with him then. This conversation was not a one-time conversation, but a topic we revisited at least once a month.

Dion knew that I was not a fan of moving in with a man before marriage and I let him know that I was not up for playing house. "I did that in Kindergarten." I told him I would move in with him if we set a firm wedding date in the Spring of 2007. He agreed but I was unsure so I prayed about it.

As I prayed, I braced myself as if the answer from God would be a big fat "No." I just knew God wasn't going to have it. The Bible was clear on this... marriage first. My Sunday school teachers were clear on this. Finally on my knees, I asked God the question and felt a peace come over me. A feeling of connection and warmth filled me. God was giving his blessing to Dion and me.

I told Dion that I had prayed on the question. "And?" Dion asked without much hope in his voice.

"God answered." I told him. "I will live with you in Florida and start our life together. We can get married the next spring."

"We could elope now." Dion offered.

"I'm from Nashville. You don't elope unless you have something to hide. We'll have a destination wedding on the beach with bridesmaids and groomsmen and your nieces will be the flower girls."

He was elated. I was happy that God allowed me to feel at peace with my decision. When people would ask me what I was going to do after graduation from NYU, I would say, "I am going to Disney World!" People assumed I meant for a two week vacation to celebrate, but what I really meant was that I was going to find my prince and my fantasy life. Not fantasy as in untrue, fantasy as in fantastic, so incredible as to stretch the mind's ability to grasp all the beauty and promise in it. "You do realize that this means you will finally have to meet my family." I told him.

"I'm looking forward to meeting your family." He insisted, despite the fact that in the two years we had been seeing each other he had failed to make the three hour drive from Atlanta to Nashville even once. I think to Dion, and to a lot of men, meeting the parents is going to the doctor, you put it off for as long as you can.

"Besides," he went on. "I'll meet your parents at your graduation."

My graduation from New York University was coming up. My family and many close friends were planning on coming. Dion's mother was coming and now Dion was onboard. Sort of.

About a week before Dion was scheduled to come up he started acting strange. I knew it was because he was nervous about meeting my family. I asked him, but he claimed it was excitement. "I got some new shoes, new slacks, and a tie for the big day," he told me.

Still the closer it got to his departure date, the more nervous he became. He was scheduled to fly in on Saturday and as late as Friday he was threatening to boycott. I was angry. My family was here. Friends had flown up, but Dion was the only face that I really wanted to see.

He was the one who had talked me through all of my whining and complaining about classes and professors for two years. He'd been the one who listened to me talk about all of the good things that I was experiencing. He was so much a part of my experience that if he weren't here with me to celebrate I would have felt like a big part of me was missing.

I woke up Saturday morning not certain if he were coming or not. Mid-morning he called to say that he had landed. I was happy that he made it even though I wasn't sure how he was going to be with my family. He called a little later to say that he had made it to his hotel and was going to get something to eat. His mom called me shortly after that and told me that she had also made it in.

I went over to the hotel where my parents were staying and sat with them and some other family friends for a little bit. Dion called and asked me to come over to his hotel.

I walked over. The first thing Dion did was give me a hug. "I'm sorry for the way I've been acting."

I accepted his apology, kissed him and we walked to the restaurant where his mother and stepfather were dining. We chatted for a minute with them and then Dion and I walked back to my parents' hotel. I told him that most of the family was at a play so he didn't have to meet everybody at one time. That made him feel a little better.

My mom answered our knock on the hotel room door, then Dion met my brother, Michele, India and Charles. We chilled in the hotel room for a couple of hours and then decided to go see the lights of Times Square. It was chilly. Dion gave me his jacket as we were walking. I snuggled in under his arm and wished that he had been with me all two years in this city.

As we were returning to the hotel, we ran into my father coming toward us with cousins, aunts and uncles in tow. The play was over and it was time to get my party started. When we got back to the hotel room, everyone fixed themselves a plate and we began to talk and laugh. The party was rocking along, when over the bedlam a booming male voice called out, "Dion, come join us."

Everything got real quiet. A half dozen of my adult male relatives sitting at a round table were motioning for Dion to join them. Dion walked over. They fixed him a drink and began to direct some pointed questions at him. Who was his family? What were his plans? What were his intentions toward their niece, cousin, sister and daughter?

I wasn't allowed at the round table discussion, but every now and then I would look over and see him smiling and laughing. One of my Aunts finally rescued him from the grilling. He shot me a grin as he stood up and walked away. "I made it out alive." He seemed to be saying to me. I was so proud of him.

The next morning we took a walk alongside the East River. He told me that he enjoyed meeting my family. "You're more like the men in your family than the women." He told me. He could see where my quick wit came from but then again he said he could see the nurturing side of me from the women in my life.

He told me that he loved me, however, he wished that there was something higher than love that he could tell me because that is what he felt. I said, "Well since there isn't, I love, love, love, love you!"

And he said, "I love, love, love, love you too." We laughed at each other's willingness to be goofy and corny and gave each other a hug and kiss. That moment was such a gift to ourselves. Vulnerable. Intimate. We'd spent two years unwrapping our hearts from the past and our fears, and now, here we were, unmasked, and in love.

We got on the F train and headed to meet his mom at the hotel and then went to the hotel where my parents were staying so that we could have brunch. Most of my family went back to their hotel rooms to get ready for another play after eating. Michele, India, Dion and I took in some of the popular landmarks in New York City. We went from Times Square to Bryant Park. Dion said that he was going to buy me something from Tiffany's. Was I ever excited! Then he said, "But I want to get you something else too, Baby."

Something more than Tiffany's? I love being spoiled but I didn't expect any of this from him. He asked me what else I wanted and I couldn't think of anything else.

Dion said, "I know what you want."

I said, "Oh really and how do you know what I want?"

"You want a Build-A-Bear."

You would have thought I had won the lottery. I was so excited, "YES!" I exclaimed, "That is what I want."

We practically raced to the Build-A-Bear workshop. Inside, Dion and I walked together through the store picking out the parts of my bear. He chose the softest bear. He chose a bear that had a small recorder to play back special messages. Dion recorded a message for me, but wouldn't let me hear it until we finished the entire bear building process. I picked out the clothes for the bear and we decided to name him DJ. When we finished putting this bear together, I pushed DJ's hand. I heard Dion's voice say, "Baby, congratulations I love you."

From Build-A-Bear we headed towards Rockefeller Center which is encased by the wonderful shopping on 5th Ave. We stopped and looked in the St. Patrick's Cathedral because the building is just so beautiful. Next we stood outside of Trump Towers, taking the "You're Fired" pictures.

Last stop, Tiffany's! When we got inside we went directly to the diamond floor. I just wanted to look. Then we went up to the silver floor where I found my necklace. It was simple and nice.

By this time, we had to go back to the hotel and get ready for dinner. Dion went to his hotel and I went to the hotel where my parents were staying to get ready. The restaurant wasn't far from either hotel but Dion called me on my cell phone to see where I was. The closer I got I could see him standing on the sidewalk waiting for me. We didn't take our eyes off of each other. You would have thought that we had been separated for years as oppose to just minutes. We embraced and he picked me up off the ground and turned me around.

Dinner was at a lovely restaurant, Chez Josephine named after Josephine Baker. I was surrounded by loved ones. Dion wandered around the table as if he didn't know where he was going to sit. I grabbed his hand and told him to sit down across from me.

I was too excited to eat but from what I can remember the food was great. At one point, my cousin leaned over and asked me if there were wedding plans in my future. I told her to ask Dion. He looked at me with a big smile and said, "Yes."

She told me to have my wedding in 2007 and hers would be in 2008. "No problem," I told her. Everything was really nice. One of my father's friends got up and sang a song. The party kept going until midnight.

Early the next morning Dion had to fly back to Orlando. I rode with him to the airport. When I got back I put on my cap and gown for graduation which was being held at Radio City Music Hall. There were traditional elements to the ceremony but it was laced with singing and dancing to Broadway show tunes. At one point, I looked back to see where my family was sitting and I saw my Dad just beaming. As I was waiting for my name to be called to walk across the stage and receive my diploma, Dion sent me an 'I love you' text message which meant more than the songs and the speeches.

Dion called me later that night and asked me how my day went. He told me that he missed me. He said that he had a great time that weekend and he apologized for waiting so long to meet my family. He also informed me that his mom's jeweler was in New York City. He said that I needed to get my ring finger sized the next day. I couldn't believe it.

The next day I went to the jeweler. I took Dion along via cell phone. He had picked the ring he liked, but he wouldn't tell me which one it was. He was trying to keep from influencing me. I picked out an A. Jaffe 1/2 carat diamond, white gold ring. It turned out to be the one Dion liked too.

Dion told me that he needed to ask my father for my hand in marriage.

"Call him," I told him.

This made him extremely nervous, I knew and he knew that if it were up to him my father would never get called, so he asked me to call my father and ask my father if he would not mind calling him so that he could do it without malingering.

I thought that it was the strangest request. My father thought that this was a strange request also, but he did it anyway. They spoke and then Dion called me. He told me that my father had said that he wasn't going to stand in the way of love and he granted Dion permission to wed his daughter. We were so excited! Later that night Dion sent me the sweetest email I had ever received.

5/11/06 to you with much love

hey, I just got home and I have been thinking of you. I wanted to write you before I called. Anyway I am very proud of you and I can't seem to get you off of my mind and truly don't want to. I wish that I could have felt and acted the way I do now because you have always deserved it and you deserved no less but the best but I am happy that I am showing you now that my love for you is true and real and I will and want to be the best husband friend lover and confidant I love your smile the way you talk the way you look into my eye's the way you hug me the way you push me to be a better person the way you can love so many people and yet I don't feel left out it takes a lot to put up with my shit and you did it and now it is my turn to always remember that and to continue to let you know that it means a lot and to do everything I can do to provide and to love and to take care of you and to make sure that you stay happy and in love with me. I LOVE YOU SO DON'T STOP LOVING ME!

The next day he wrote me the following email:

5/12/06 love

> *I remember a time when you asked me what love means to me and I played it off but now I will tell you and I say that love is a true feeling that few people have a chance to feel it is satisfying warm and unconditional and everlasting it is really explainable I can say it is what I feel for you this is a little of what love is and means to me I will show and tell you more*
>
> *I love you xoxoxoxoxoxoxoxoxoxoxoxoxoxo.!*

"We keep moving forward, opening new doors, and doing new things, because we're curious and curiosity keeps leading us down new paths."

-*Walt Disney*

CHAPTER THIRTEEN

Moving in the Direction of Love

I couldn't wait to move to Florida! I told Dion that I needed to at least go home to Tennessee for a week and celebrate Mother's Day with my mom and spend some time with the family. He could come to Tennessee on the next Saturday then we could drive down together on Sunday.

When I arrived on Saturday my mom was surprised because I had told her that I wasn't going to be able to come home. My parents were not aware at that point of my decision to move to Florida. I had delayed telling them because I knew that they would not be happy about me moving in with Dion.

I finally broke the news over dinner and the questions flowed. Had I lost my mind? Was I doing it out of love or lust? I was accused of being disobedient towards God. My mother told me that if I wanted to see him every once in a while that would be fine; however, to live with him was not okay.

They blamed my desire to live with a man before marriage on people who had also "shacked up" in and outside of my family. They were disappointed and unsure of how to deal with me.

That Sunday as I was sitting in church listening to the music and the message, I had a vision. In my mind, I saw Dion walking up to the front of the church as a symbol of giving his life to Christ. I thought now wouldn't that be nice but I knew that

Dion was very shy and that walking up to the front of the church was a long shot.

Joy had come to Nashville for a conference that week. I met her for lunch. She gave me a graduation gift and I gave her a Mother's Day present. I enjoyed sharing that time with her. She told me that she was happy that I was in her son's life. I told her I was happy to be in his life.

When I was leaving the hotel, I got a call from the jeweler. He told me that the prong setting for the ring couldn't fit the diamond. He wanted to know if I had to have that exact ring. I asked why a half carat diamond wouldn't fit in the prong setting. He told me that the diamond was actually a full carat.

"Oh," I said, "I didn't know that."

He asked me to look at some other rings and let him know what I liked as soon as I could. I hung up and called Dion more than a little excited. He was disappointed that I knew the actual size of the stone. He was giving me the diamond that his mother had given him a few years ago. That night I got on the internet and started looking at other rings. With Dion on the phone, we emailed websites links to each other. We were excited and couldn't wait for the weekend to be together when Dion would fly in so that we could drive to Orlando together.

That Saturday I had planned a fun filled day for Dion. I got some sub sandwiches and chips and drinks then I picked him up from the Nashville airport. I'd bought a picnic basket earlier that week and I put all of the food in the basket. We went to the park and had a picnic by the pond. Then I showed him around Nashville. We went to the mall and then we drove to my parent's house. They were on their way to a wedding. They were also upset because they had expected us to get there earlier so they could have gotten to know the man I was planning on spending my life with a little better.

The next morning in church, Dion was sitting to the left of me in the pew. The pastor extended the invitation to Christian discipleship. I looked over to my right to get a pen out of my purse and when I turned back Dion was walking down the aisle, looking back and flashing me the brightest smile.

I didn't know what to think. My vision was coming true. I went up to the front of the church and gave him a big hug. As I walked back to my seat, the first lady of the church reached over and whispered to me, "I am so happy for you."

I was happy for Dion, but I wanted to know what compelled him to walk up there. Maybe it was none of my business, but I really wanted to know. After church I introduced Dion to my church family and then we left.

We went back to the house my mother cooked dinner while I finished packing. We ate and then I went to my room to get my things to put in the car.

My parents came down the hall and my father offered to pray. Even though my father was a deacon at the church, I wasn't sure that I wanted him to pray for us because he wasn't happy about my decision and I knew that I would be able to feel that in his prayer. I don't remember the exact prayer; however, I know it had to do with him not being happy and me making my own decisions. I do not think that prayer is supposed to be that uncomfortable.

My brother offered to help take some of my bags to the car. When we finished loading we said our final goodbyes and walked to the car. I could tell that Dion was worrying about me. He said, "Baby, thank you for loving me."

"You're welcome, but why are you thanking me for that now?" I asked.

"Because I know how much you love your family and they don't want you to leave, but you did it for me," he replied.

"No, I did it for us. Stop worrying about it." I said to reassure him.

As I got in the driver's seat I said, "I'll do Nashville to Atlanta because I was used to that drive and you do Atlanta to Orlando."

It wasn't an even trade but he was cool with that. Plus, I wanted him to take in the scenery of the drive from Tennessee to Georgia. It's so beautiful, looking at the black cows graze in the green fields and descending Mount Eagle looking at the green trees against the blue sky. I loved that drive. It had always been a time for me to think about things and pray and maybe even cry and laugh to myself about my life, where I was going and where I had been. Now I was taking this drive with the man I loved and we talked about where we had been and where we were going.

As we were driving along I asked him what made him go up to the front of the church. He slowly looked at me and said, "I see you and you're so happy all of the time and you're not worried about things and I wanted what you have."

I hadn't known he felt that way. He'd spoken to his father earlier that week and told his father how much he loved me and wanted me to be his wife, His father told him that if he really loved me then he should put God first. Dion said that he wanted us to go to church and make sure that we put God first in our relationship.

The hours and miles brought us closer to Atlanta. A thought occurred to me. Dion's brother and sister-in-law had just had a baby boy that we hadn't seen yet. "We should stop by and say hi to your brother and his family," I told him.

"Really? We don't have to," he said as though he felt it would be an inconvenience.

"Yeah, but we should," I said thinking about how important family was to both of us.

We stopped at his Mom's house first. I told her that Dion had walked to the front of the church to give his life to Christ. She was happy for him and happy for us.

We left her house and headed to his brother's apartment. Everyone was happy to see him. He and his brother went outside and talked for a while. I sat inside and played with his nieces and nephew and spoke to his sister-in-law. We chilled there for about an hour and then we got back on the road.

As we were pulling off from the apartment, I put the car in drive and Dion looked at me, "Thank you for letting me spend time with my family."

"Our family." I corrected him.

He smiled and said, "I love you."

It was early morning when we arrived at Dion's apartment. We emptied the car and made the bed with fresh sheets. I called my mom to let her know that we had made it safely.

When I got off the phone, I got in bed and closed my eyes. Dion got in beside me, and said, "Aren't we supposed to be praying together?" I looked at him and nodded. He took my hand. I prayed for him and then he prayed for me.

We went out that next afternoon. He showed me where the nearest grocery stores were and where the closest mall was located. By the time we got back to the apartment it was time for him to go to school.

I waved good-bye and went inside our apartment. My mother called to tell me how upset my father was and how he was blaming other people for my decision to "shack up." Her tone was unhappy, nevertheless, she didn't say anything about her feelings.

I called Dion to tell him. I wasn't trying to worry him, but I should have known better. When he got home that night, he looked terrible. I could tell he was upset. He just looked at me and shook his head. I asked him what was wrong.

"I don't want you to leave me."

"Why would I leave you? What is wrong?" We were standing in the kitchen and he was leaning against the sink trying not to look at me. I could tell that he was about to cry.

"Because your parents don't want you to be here."

"So what does that have to do with me leaving you?"

"I don't want to be the reason that your family isn't happy. I won't like it, but I will understand if you go back home, so that your parents won't be mad at you."

I took his face in my hands and made him look me in the eyes. "I don't want to be in Nashville, I want to be with you. Baby, I am not going anywhere."

He blinked back a tear. "Besides," I continued, " I just got here, why would I go away? I am a grown woman. I have a Bachelor's Degree and a Master's Degree and I'm in love with a thick headed man who happens to live in Florida. So here I am."

CHAPTER FOURTEEN

Kiss me

When Saturday came we wanted to go somewhere fun. We couldn't afford Disney World or Universal Studios, yet there was a more affordable place that I had gone to when I was a little girl, a reptile themed park name Gatorland. Known as the Alligator Capital of the World, Gatorland is a 110-acre theme park and nature conservatory located at the head of the Florida Everglades.

It was a beautiful Florida day. We walked around and looked at the different snakes of Florida in the cages. There was also a huge alligator that had been captured and moved here because it had ventured to close to civilization and gotten into the habit of dining on neighborhood pets.

There were a lot of shows throughout the day featuring trainers and animals. The first show we went to was called "Upclose Encounters." We sat in stadium style bleacher seats, close enough to see; yet, not so close that we might be picked to "volunteer" to be part of the show.

On the stage were various size wooden boxes. Sure enough, the trainer started by asking for volunteers who were ushered on stage to stand by the boxes. Once the volunteers were assembled the trainer asked them to close their eyes and hold out their hands.

Stopping at the first volunteer, the trainer pulled two six inch black scorpions from the box and put one in each palm.

When the volunteer opened her eyes, she looked a little frightened; and yet, she handled herself better than I would have. I think I would have bolted after tossing the bugs sky high.

I turned to Dion and said, "Baby, you should have gone up there, you're not afraid of a little scorpion." He smiled and looked at me like I was crazy.

The boxes got bigger. So did the critters inside. For the last box they asked for three volunteers. Somehow they got them. These three volunteers took their positions and closed their eyes. When they opened them they were holding an eight foot yellow boa constrictor.

We applauded the trainer and volunteers and found something to eat. When we were done we ventured out on the Swamp Walk. It was nothing spectacular just a nice nature walk where the trees provided shade. It was just me and Dion. It was peaceful.

We made our way to the observation tower that looked out over the swampland. At the top of the stairs, we could see out over an expanse of the swamp. Giant white egrets perched high in Cyprus trees. We could look down into the murky water full of alligators and crocodiles. As we stood, arm in arm, raindrops began to fall.

"The sky falls out at the same time every day." Dion told me looking up at a few measly clouds dropping the rain.

We stood there for a moment and watched the rain sweep across the swamp water. The sun was still beaming brightly, it was beautiful, all these forces of nature working together to create a spectacular scene.

As we were leaving the park, I thought about Epcot and Universal Studios and the spectacular attractions those parks have. I realized it would not have been the same kind of afternoon if we had gone to one of those parks. Dion and I would have been distracted by the sounds and lights and noise. Here at Gatorland, we were the main attraction for each other.

When we got back to the house Dion saw a post office notice on the door. He was upset about it. "Man, I missed it."

I played dumb as if I didn't know what he was so upset about but I knew that the mail man had tried to deliver my ring. I also knew that the next day was Sunday and the day after was Memorial Day and there would be no mail, no ring for at least forty eight hours.

"Two days," Dion fretted. "I can't wait two days."

"Wait two days for what?" I asked innocently. Yet, I couldn't keep a straight face.

He grabbed me around the waist and said jokingly, "Two days before I can give you a ring and make you an honest woman, or at least try. God knows it will not be easy."

I squirmed to get away, but he held me tightly. "When I get the ring on Monday…" he began to say.

"Tuesday," I corrected him. "No mail on Memorial Day."

His face dropped and I could see his disappoint. "Tuesday," he said as though it was a million years away. "Should I give you the ring in the morning before school or at night when I get home?"

"Let's wait until you get home so that we can celebrate," I said with a huge smile on my face and anticipation in my voice.

The weekend dragged on with Dion checking the mailbox twice more even though he knew that the post office was on holiday. We got in the bed Monday night and I set my alarm so that he could get up and go to the post office as soon as it opened. We said our prayers and put heads on our pillows; however, Dion tossed and turned all night like a kid at Christmas waiting for Santa Claus to arrive.

When the alarm went off, he jumped up like a fireman, threw on some clothes, and raced out the door. I went back to sleep. After a little while I heard him come in. He went into the den first.

He came into the bedroom and got back in the bed. His body was cool and his heart was thumping. I snuggled up to him and he laid there holding me for a second, and only a second, before he said, "Baby, can I just give you the ring now?"

"Not now, I'm sleepy," I said it in a teasing voice and with a smile that sent him running into the den. He flew back into the bedroom, sliding into the side of the bed on one knee like a baseball player sliding into home base. He looked at me with a twinkle in his eyes and said in a loving voice, "Angela, I love you. Will you marry me?"

My hair was a mess. I didn't have my contacts in or my glasses on and morning breath permeated the air. I was thinking that I could at least brush my teeth. Instead I sat up, straightened my hair and pajamas and then looked at him slowly and said, "Could you repeat the question?"

He scooted closer to me and slid the ring on my finger. "Will you marry me?"

I looked into those brown eyes. "Yes, of course, I will."

The ring on my finger was beautiful; and yet, even more beautiful was this man who loved me.

I didn't want Dion to go to school that morning. I wanted to celebrate, but I knew he had to go. I stayed home and called my friends and family and told them that I was officially engaged. I called my parents first out of respect; however, no one answered.

I took pictures of the ring and emailed them to some friends. Dion called and asked how I was doing. He did that every day, but today was a little different. I knew that he couldn't wait to get home. I asked him if we could go out and celebrate and he said that we would not be able to tonight but maybe on the weekend.

When he got home, his story had changed. "Get dressed. We're going out to celebrate," he said excitedly. We went to a seafood restaurant. I had oysters for my appetizer. He had jalapeño poppers. He didn't normally like oysters, but he saw how I was preparing mine and asked to try it. I took a saltine cracker, placed an oyster on top and dolloped some cocktail sauce on that and fed it to him. He really enjoyed it, but not as much as I did. Perhaps it was the fragrance of engagement in the air which made him a little fonder of the mollusks than he was before. We ordered a fried seafood platter and some cocktails to toast our new journey. As we shared our food and toasted our pending nuptials, we felt connected in a way we never had before. We were really beginning a new adventure.

Exactly a week later, the lead story in the local news was about a man who had been riding on a motorcycle behind a minivan. The guy in the van had abruptly slammed on his brakes. The guy on the motorcycle had not. He crashed into the van's bumper and catapulted over the handlebars and through the rear windshield of the minivan.

For some reason, the guy in the minivan kept driving with this man hanging out of the back window. There was no video of this, but in my mind's eye I saw the van maneuvering through the city streets with a pair of kicking legs protruding through the shattered glass.

Eventually the van pulled over and the motorcycle rider was pretty much okay. He was shown being interviewed at a hospital, sitting up in his bed and talking to the TV reporter.

I turned off the television, spun around to Dion, and declared, "I'm driving you to school tomorrow and not just because of the man and the van, but also because tomorrow is Tuesday."

"Tuesday?" he looked at me with a baffled expression on his face.

I looked at him shocked that he didn't realize the significance of the day and began to explain it to him. "Tuesday, June 6th, 2006, or numerically, six-six-0 six." I hit the last six with special emphasis.

"It's just another day," he replied in an unconcerned and matter fact voice.

"Unh-uh. Six-six-oh-six and you know what happens then," I replied.

"Umm, all hell breaks loose? ' he said in his most sarcastic voice.

"No. *The Omen IV* is opening in theaters. People are going to be spooked and out of control and I do not want you riding around Orlando impaled in the back of some maniac's van."

Dion looked at me like I was speaking in Turkish, "I'm a grown a-- man and I'll ride my bike to school if I want to."

"Grown man? You're crazy." I said even louder, "I forbid you to ride your bike tomorrow on the day the Omen comes out. You could end up stuck in a van headed to Miami."

He looked at me trying not to laugh. "I think you're right, and not only that, I think we should both stay home, all day, with no lights on, never leaving the bedroom, tucked under the covers, not even breathing too hard, unless of course we have to."

"I'm not playing around," I warned him.

"Me either," he assured me as he grabbed me in his arms and pulled me to him laughing.

I knew motorcycles weren't safe, at least not as safe as cars. The earlier accident had freaked me out; nevertheless, I understood his passion and would never have denied him something from which he got so much joy and excitement. I wish I had something that I was that excited about.

Motorcycles had been a part of Dion's life since he was nine years old. He loved the machines and the thrill of riding them with a passion. And the truth was so did I. Sitting behind Dion, arms around his chest, the feeling of freedom as we rode on twisting highways alongside the ocean was exhilarating.

The dreaded June sixth, 2006 arrived. Dion climbed on his bike and drove to school. I prayed for his safety as I did every day, but this time I was more focused because of the eeriness of the date. I was cooking dinner when he walked through the door that evening. I was so happy to see him. My prayers had been answered. He gave me a hug and a kiss.

He had a grin on his face and he told me that he had gone to buy me some flowers on his way home to replace the white flowers wilting in our vase; however, he had decided against it.

"I want to buy you something more than flowers, something that you would really like and enjoy. " He told me.

"Really?" I questioned. "What do you want to buy me?"

He looked at me with a cockeyed grin on his face and said one word. "Shoes!"

I could have fallen over. Forget Prince Charming. This was so beyond any fairytale I'd ever read or heard of. A man wanting to buy me shoes? I thought to myself, "Nobody pinch me, if I'm dreaming let me dream!"

This was a big leap from his previous sentiment regarding the purchase of shoes. "My dad told me," Dion he said once, "That if you buy a woman shoes, she will either walk all over you or she'll walk out on you."

I told him that that was crazy talk. "Dion, if you buy me shoes, I'll just look good in my new shoes next to you."

The impetus behind this shopping trip was a check that his Step-mother had mailed him. He hadn't been that close to her even though she was continually kind to him. He was so happy that she was reaching out to him and wanting to help him.

He wanted to go to the mall immediately, but I hadn't finished cooking and I was hungry. I knew that if I got too hungry I would be irritable; nonetheless he was a man on a shoe mission. He said that we could get a snack at the mall.

The mall had five different stores specializing in women's shoes. We started at the south end and started working our way north. I can be particular about shoes and the first two stores were disappointments.

Dion grabbed my hand and we walked to an athletic shoe store. I was surprised by Dion's determination to buy me some shoes. I saw some Pumas that I liked; however, they didn't have my size. We left there and went to another athletic shoe store. Although I saw another nice pair of Pumas, they didn't have my size in that one either. We did not do any better at the last store we visited. We gave up. Even a good man can only shop for women's shoes for so long.

In the car on the way home, our conversation wandered from shoes to stepmothers to ice cream and then strangely we began talking about death. Dion looked at me at one point very solemnly. "When I die," he told me, "I want to be buried rather than cremated. If God intends for me to burn then He will send me to hell."

When we got home, I finished cooking dinner. We ate and I'm not sure what happened, but I felt this twinge of insecurity. It was as if he was hiding something from me again. I think it was triggered by a visit from his female neighbor who I had just met when she unexpectedly stopped by the apartment. While she was petting Cujo, Dion's puppy, she said, "He still pees every time you pet him." Although she laughed, I failed to find anything funny, least of all the fact that she knew that.

Her statement struck me as too familiar. Dion had told me that he had never let a female into his apartment. According to him, only his boys came over. I asked him about that claim again and his response was that she was like one of the boys which was why he hadn't mentioned her.

I told him that if she wasn't that big of a deal, then why not tell me about her before now. Even though he thought that I was blowing things out of proportion, and maybe I was, I wanted to know the truth. Instead of continuing the conversation, I fled into the bathroom and got in the shower. Dion came in and asked me to calm down.

I wanted to ask him if he'd been with another woman at any time during our relationship, but I stopped myself. He walked out of the bathroom. I got out of the shower and dried myself off. He called out from the living room that the movie was ready.

Once I got dressed, I went back in and we watched the movie, *Wedding Crashers*. The title seemed somewhat ironic. I sat in the big king chair. He sat on the floor in front of me. We didn't talk or laugh much. As the credits rolled, Dion got up to go to bed. "Good night," he said as he walked away.

I sat there and stared at the TV screen. What was this state that I was in? Why was I feeling this way? No explanation I could think of made much sense to me. Finally, I went to bed. Dion held out his arms to hug me and we kissed. I still get chills from that kiss. It was the most passionate I have ever experienced. It was as if his kiss was saying that he loved me and there was nothing I could do about it. .

He could tell I was still distant so he asked, "What is going on with you?"

I told him that I had this feeling that he had cheated on me. I wasn't sure where it came from, but I still had it. He told me that he had never cheated. Then he asked if I had ever wanted to cheat on him. I assured him that thought never really crossed my mind.

We went back and forth pecking at each other. Wanting reassurance and so afraid to accept it when it was offered. My mask was back. It got late. We talked less and finally fell asleep. Neither one of us had any way to know that this was the last night we would ever spend together on earth.

CHAPTER FIFTEEN

Serious...

The next morning I woke up before Dion. I didn't get out of the bed. I just laid there slowly taking in the day. Dion had hung a maroon sheet as a curtain so that the sun would not wake us up before we were ready. The way the ripples in the sheet fell, and the way the sunlight was coming through blinds made the sheet look like it had slanted eyes, a long nose and a ghoulish smile - like a demonic face.

I blinked hoping that the sleep in my eyes was playing tricks on me. I opened them again. The demonic face was still there. I put my arms around Dion a little afraid. The sheet had been up for at least five days and had never gone over to the dark side before. Today, though, it had turned. It freaked me out.

Dion began to wake up. I asked him to look at the sheet, "Doesn't it look like a scary face?"

He stared at it for a second before answering. "Yes, it does," he said.

He got out of the bed and let Cujo out of his cage to go relieve himself. He brought him back in and then started getting ready for school. He went into the bathroom and I went into the kitchen to fix myself a glass of juice.

The tension from last night was still between us. While he was in the bathroom, I knocked on the door. He pulled the door open and he looked up at me with his eyebrows raised as if to say, "What do you want?" I wasn't trying to annoy him.

"Do you want me to fix you something for lunch?"

He shook his head and said, "No."

Before I could turn to walk away the bathroom door closed firmly. I was usually the one who closed the bathroom door and took sanctuary in the bathroom. I was the one who liked to be alone to ponder and question what life is all about. But today was different.

I got on the computer. I opened email and began to read. A few minutes later, Dion came out of the bathroom and went into the kitchen for his vitamins. I was hoping that he wasn't so upset that I wouldn't get my usual kiss goodbye. He came out of the kitchen into the den and looked at me for a second, then leaned down and gave me a kiss. I smiled and walked him to the door. "Have a good day, Baby," I told him.

"You, too."

I closed it behind him then listened as his motorcycle engine started and then faded away into the distance. And suddenly a thought drifted into my mind, "What if this is the last time I see him?"

I had to pull myself together. What in the world was I thinking? He wasn't going to leave me again. We were in love and people that are in love have arguments and disagreements and miscommunications all of the time. God knows the last two years were proof of that. He wasn't going to leave me.

I didn't have much planned for the day. I needed to run a few errands and go by the grocery store to buy veggies for dinner. This thought of buying groceries was immediately followed by an inner voice. You don't need to buy groceries for dinner tonight.

I'd had general feelings of uneasiness over the past few months, but this was a specific voice. No need to buy groceries. It rattled me. I paced around the apartment and then decided some normal activity would calm me down.

I went to the gas station and filled up before heading toward the grocery store. On the way, my cell phone rang. I was hoping that it was Dion, but it was my friend Anne. I hadn't talked to her much since I'd been in Florida so I was happy to hear her voice. I told her that I was on my way to buy groceries for dinner. She made some silly comment about me being all domestic now.

"I know it is crazy, but I enjoy cooking for him." I was still on the phone with her when I reached the grocery store. I got out of the car. The hot Florida summer wind hit my face and I felt that feeling again. You don't need to buy food for dinner.

I didn't tell Anne, I just kept talking to her. She told me that she had to go and would call me back. I hung up the phone and hustled for the air conditioned store.

I wasn't sure what I wanted to cook, but I figured I would get inspired as I shopped. The previous Sunday the pastor had challenged the congregation to try the Daniel fast, so Dion and I decided to take him up on the challenge. I knew that I would have a lot more vegetables in my cart than I normally would. Dion and I both loved broccoli, so I grabbed a stalk of that. I grabbed a few sweet potatoes because we both liked them, too. I picked up a bag salad and on the way to checkout, I passed the greeting card section. I browsed until I found one especially for Dion.

As I was putting the groceries in the car that eerie feeling came back. I heard a voice say, "I told you not to buy groceries, and you chose not to listen." I'm not one who puts a lot of stock in voices and premonitions. I don't believe in fortune tellers or psychics; however, this voice was bothering me. I got in my car and drove back to the apartment.

The broccoli and salad went in the refrigerator. I left the other things on the counter. Dion wouldn't be home for three hours so I figured I would start cooking later. I took Cujo outdoors. We played for a little bit and then I put him back in his cage. It was very hot that day. It seemed as though the sun had taken a needle and drained all of the energy out of my body. I felt exhausted; so I went into the bedroom with the card I'd picked out for Dion. I sat on the side of the bed and wrote:

Baby,

I'm not sure of what I should write. I just want you to know that I don't mean to do things or say things that question my sincerity in this relationship. There are things that I have not told you about, because I have forgotten their relevance and those things are not at the forefront of my mind.

What is at the forefront of my heart and my mind is how much I love you, how much I pray that God helps us to get through our rough patches and blesses us. I thank God for making you the loving heart that he made you. You're a beautiful person inside and out.

Thank you for loving me despite my craziness at times. We are starting something new and we still have a lot to learn about each other.

Love Always Your Sweet Pea

After I finished writing, I put the card in the envelope and placed it in between the keys on the keyboard of the computer. I figured that the computer would be a good place to put it because I knew that he would be able to see it as soon as he sat down to check his email.

I went back into the bedroom, kicked off my flip flops and dropped onto the bed. As I was preparing to take a nap, my phone rang. It was Dion... Finally! I had been waiting on him to call me.

"Hey, Baby," he said. "I decided to call you because I figured you were too stubborn to call me."

I knew he was right. I knew that I could be stubborn and I I needed to work on that. I told him that I figured he was mad at me and he just needed some time. "And besides," I defended myself, "you usually call me when you get to school to let me know that you made it there safely."

I asked him how his day was going. His voice pitched higher and I could tell that I was in for a bad day story. "Man, my teacher tried to take off three of my fingers."

He went on to tell me that the teacher had been demonstrating how a part worked. He'd asked Dion to volunteer to hold the part. Somehow, the way Dion was holding it could have cost Dion his fingers. Dion was pissed and rightfully so.

The counselor in me came out. I assured him that he should be pissed, but I also asked him to calm down. His line beeped. It was his mother. "Baby, this is my mom. I will call you back. I love you."

"I love you, too."

He clicked off. I fell back on the bed and it didn't take long for sleep to take over. I slept solidly and it was a struggle to wake up. The more I tried to rouse myself, the more I drifted back toward an unconscious state. When I finally got my eyes fully open, I felt a little dizzy. I looked at the clock. It was late. Dion would be home very soon. "Got to start dinner now," I thought to myself.

As I walked into the kitchen, I heard, "why would you start cooking now after I have told you all day that you don't need to prepare anything for dinner?" That damn feeling and voice AGAIN! What was this…paranoia? I refused to listen so I went into the kitchen anyway. However, the feeling stayed with me even after I began to cook. A new question entered into my mind. Was this feeling my friend or my foe? I didn't know the answer so I decided to continue to cook.

I turned the oven on and ran water over the potatoes. While I was washing them, the eerie feeling seemed to flow away. My cell phone rang. It was my friend Michele. She was calling to check on me. I told her that I was in the process of cooking dinner.

"Where is Dion? Shouldn't he be home by now?"

Before I answered her, I looked at the clock. It was late for him. "Yeah, he should be," I said. "Maybe he stopped, for gas or something."

We continued talking until my line beeped. I looked at the phone and it read Ms. Joy. "That's strange," I thought. Why is Dion's mother calling me? I clicked over, and said "Hello?"

"Hi, Angela. Are you sitting down?" I could hear the concern in her voice.

"Should I be?" I asked even as I walked over to the chair in front of the computer and sat.

"Dion has been in an accident." The exact words that I didn't want to hear somehow came churning through the phone. "He's at the hospital. I have the number for you to call."

She proceeded to tell me the name of the person that I would be contacting, Robert. "Call him and get to the hospital. I'm going to catch a flight out as soon as I can."

I hung up and called Robert. I told him that I was Dion's fiancé and that I'd just gotten off the phone with Dion's mother. He asked me, "How soon can you get here?"

"I guess it depends on traffic, but I will get there as soon as I can. How bad is he?" I asked.

"It's serious."

The word 'serious' ran through my head. What did he mean by 'serious'? A broken arm? A leg? Worse?

Robert told me that he would meet me in the Emergency Room waiting area. I turned off the oven, grabbed my keys and purse and ran. From the car, I called Anne to ask her if she would pray for Dion but she didn't answer. I began to pray by myself.

I prayed that he'd still be alive. I prayed that I would get there without having an accident myself. Thankfully, there wasn't too much traffic.

At this point, it wasn't that hot. I didn't feel drained. There were no more voices. And although I knew that it was serious, whatever that meant, I remember looking at the palm trees swaying in the wind, the sunshine beaming like a bright smile as it was slowly dropping from the sky, and the blue sky with a horizon that seemed to go on forever. I was captivated by the physical beauty of the Florida landscape and scenery surrounding me. No matter how serious it was, all I could think was that it was such a beautiful picturesque day. What a contradiction.

CHAPTER SIXTEEN
I See You (ICU)

The beautiful scenery seemed to help me get to my destination much more quickly. When I looked up, I had finally arrived at the hospital. I called Robert when I pulled into the ER parking lot but he didn't answer. I walked inside concerned, lost, and not knowing what to expect. I was looking for Robert, who was a stranger, to guide me to the person with whom I was probably most intimate, my love. I immediately sought out someone who could tell me where Dion was, so I approached the woman behind the information desk. Frustratingly enough, she did not show a Dion Miller in her computer. I asked her if she knew someone by the name of Robert. She didn't. I was back to square one. I had finally made it to the hospital and still couldn't get to Dion.

I walked back outside. My cell phone rang. It was Robert. I told him that I was outside about to walk back in. He told me that he would meet me there. I walked in and saw a man coming towards me in a coat and tie. His face looked long as though he had seen many sad days and had to report on each them. I wasn't sure I was reading him correctly, but once he extended his hand and told me his title, it all made sense. "I'm Robert, the hospital chaplain," he said. I thought to myself, "The chaplain, my God this is serious."

Robert walked me upstairs to a waiting room where a receptionist sat. When I approached him looking for Dion, he told me that he had no record of a Dion Miller in his database either. However, he did have a John Doe who had been admitted to ICU.

Upon receiving that information, I decided to call Dion's mother, Joy, however, she didn't answer. I left a message to let her know that I was at the hospital, but I hadn't heard anything else regarding Dion's condition. Upon hanging up, my phone rang. It was Jess, Dion's sister-in- law. I couldn't get a good signal and the call dropped so I went down the hallway to an alcove that had ceiling to floor windows thinking I might get a signal there.

Before I could call Jess back, my phone rang again. It was a number that I didn't recognize. I hesitantly answered it anyway. Although I didn't recognize the voice it was evident that they were trying to reach me. "Hello, Angela. This is Dr. Miller, Dion's father," said a male voice that was trembling but trying to stay strong.

My heart started racing. I'd never spoken to Dr. Miller before or even heard his voice. Dion and his father were not close but had recently begun rekindling their relationship. I hated that this had to be our first conversation. I often imagined meeting Dr. Miller over dinner with Dion introducing me as his fiancé. Even though it was not an ideal situation for us to meet, I could hear the concern he had for his son. He asked me how Dion was doing.

"I just got to the hospital. I haven't seen Dion or a doctor yet," I told him. He responded almost with a sigh of relief. Even though I didn't have good news, the fact that I didn't have any news was our only comfort. He asked me to call him when I received an update about Dion's condition. When I finished our conversation, I called Jess back. I told her that I hadn't heard anything yet. She told me that Joy was on her way to the airport and that Joy wanted me to call her when I got any information.

I asked her how Dion's brother Tommy was doing. "Not good," she told me.

When I hung up, I looked through the window to a courtyard with plush greenery and flowers. The building blocked the direct sunlight creating a shaded garden. I imagined that there was a cool breeze in that shade. I wanted to step out into it; however, on this side of my imagination I was under fluorescent lights waiting for news about my fiancé. A realization came over me. I'm his only family in Florida and the only thing I can do right now is wait.

I needed help. I needed God to be there with me. I called my brother because I knew he would pray for me. He didn't answer his phone. I left him a message telling him that Dion had been in a motorcycle accident and asking him to please pray for him. Next, I called my parents. I didn't know how they were going to respond, but I wanted them to know that I was scared and that I just needed their love.

My mom answered on the third ring. I told her that Dion had been in a bad accident. She told me that she was sorry to hear that. "Do you want me to come down?" she asked. "Yes," I told her. Even though conversations had been strained at the time, I wanted my mother.

I headed back down the hall to the waiting room. When I walked through the door, the receptionist told me that the doctor had come up to see me, but no one knew where I was.

I told her that I had been standing in the hallway so that I could have cell phone reception. She immediately called the doctor and told me that he would be right up.

I sat down. I wasn't as afraid as I was numb. I didn't know what to expect. I knew in my heart that Dion was alive. I could feel him. I knew that they were not going to tell me "We did everything that we could," but what had happened that was 'serious'.

One of Dion's friends from the mechanics school, Ronnie, walked in. He was immediately followed by two doctors. I froze as they walked toward me. I saw Ronnie sit down in one of the chairs closest to the door. One of doctors stood right in front of me. The other doctor stood to my right. They shook my hand and told me that they had performed surgery on Dion.

The next thing they said stopped my heart. "We had to amputate his left leg."

My brain got stuck on that sentence but they kept talking. Their words came to me faint and distant as if arriving from some other world. "The left leg has a main artery and the only way to stop the bleeding was to take the leg completely."

I heard something about internal bleeding and patching up his belly. I wondered if 'belly' was an acceptable medical term and if these men really doctors?

"He's not stabilizing," the other doctor told me. "We've moved him to ICU."

The doctors walked away promising to keep me informed. Ronnie moved closer to me. He'd heard everything that the doctors had said. We began talking about how Dion would not be happy about this and how he could get a prosthetic leg. Ronnie said something about Dion not being able to drive motorcycles any more but that he could drive three or four wheelers. I knew that Dion would not be happy with that, nevertheless, I entertained the conversation anyway.

I told Ronnie I needed to call Dion's family. I went back down the hallway in front of the windows. It was darker outside now. I thought about news that I was about to deliver. I prayed for help to find the right words and the courage to say them. I called his mom first but she didn't answer. I left her message asking her to call me back. Next, I called Jess and told her what the doctors told me. She seemed to handle it calmly.

My last call was to Dr. Miller. His wife answered. I told her that they had amputated Dion's left leg and she screamed. I could feel the terror in her voice. It took her several minutes to regain control, then she said that she would inform his father.

Somehow, I hadn't expected her response. I was blocking out my own emotions hanging onto the fact he was still alive. It was my only comfort. I didn't expect him to die that was the furthest thing from my mind.

When I got back to the waiting room, my cell phone rang which surprised me because it had not been working in there the entire time I had been at the hospital. It was Joy. "Hi, Honey, sorry I missed your call. I was going through security. What did the doctor say?"

There is no easy way to tell a mother that a part of her child had been taken. My brain tried to find the softest language, but it all came to the same bottom line. "They had to amputate his left leg." I rushed on as if to erase my first words, "They patched up the internal bleeding in his belly and they are trying to stabilize him."

"But he is still alive?" she said her voice laden with exhaustion.

"Yes," I told her. "He is still alive." We exhaled together. Joy told me to be strong. She would be there soon.

I turned to Ronnie who was holding a Bible. He told me that he had recently started going to church. He had been told to start by reading a Proverb chapter a day. I appreciated his presence and his conversation. He told me that he really liked the church he was going to and that Dion and I should come with him one Sunday.

As I was partially listening to him, a part of my brain was calculating time wondering when the doctors were going to come back. My cell phone rang. It was my father. I told him the phone was acting up and to call me on the hospital phone. He called me back immediately and told me that my mother was booking a flight to leave the next morning.

A nurse came to the door. "Is anyone here a family member of Dion Miller?" I told her that I was his fiancé.

She walked over to me and asked if I would like to see him. I wasn't sure. A part of me wanted to rush to his side. Another part of me was chilled by the look on the nurse's face. I walked over to her and nodded.

She led me into the intensive care unit, but stopped before going in. She turned to face me with that look that chilled me earlier. It was as though she was unsure how to say what she had to say. Finally she simply said, "He isn't conscious and there's a lot of blood everywhere. "

I could only nod and then she led me in. I didn't notice any blood. I only saw Dion's face. He looked like he was sleeping. I didn't even think to notice the left side of his body right away. I looked at his face and there wasn't a scratch on it. "Thank God he was wearing a helmet," I thought to myself especially since you don't legally have to wear a helmet in the state of Florida.

There were two other nurses in the room monitoring the equipment. He was on a respirator and attached to an IV pumping blood into his body. Even though I turned my ears toward her, my eyes were locked on him. "The more blood we put into him, the more he pumps it out," one of the nurses told me.

I looked at her and nodded my head to acknowledge her. What was I supposed to say? I wanted Dion to know that I was there but, there were too many people for me to get close. I felt awkward and out of place, and at the same time, I felt like I was really the only person who should have been there. I knew I wasn't a doctor or a nurse, but I knew Dion and I loved him. I was the only one there who had been through the good times and the not so good times with him. I was the one who he proposed to a week ago. Yet, I was the only one not doing anything. I made my way to his side and took his hand and whispered to him, "I'm here, Baby. It's okay now." I was struck by how cold his hands were resting in mine. I wanted to warm his hands with my own even though I knew that very well might be impossible.

The nurses were busy around him. One attached a new plastic bag of blood for his transfusion. Dion never moved, never showed any sign of pain or acknowledged my presence. Yet, somehow death was still the furthest thing from my mind.

After a few minutes, I went back into the waiting room. I began to feel a pain in my throat and I knew that a stream of tears were on the way. I didn't feel strong anymore. I began crying uncontrollably .

I didn't know where these tears were coming from. I didn't want to believe that the worst that could happen. Why would God allow us to be in a long distance relationship for two years and then only allow us two weeks of us being physically together?

Ronnie's girlfriend came over to comfort me and told me that it was going to be alright. How did she know that it was going to be alright? I knew she was trying to comfort me but it wasn't her fiancé who was lying in the hospital without a left leg. I didn't feel like it was going to be alright. Dion was going to hate the way he looked. He would probably try to push me away and not believe that I actually loved him. He might think that I was sticking by him out of pity. All in all, it wasn't going to be alright!

More of his friends from school came in to the waiting room. I knew they were there to show their support, yet I still felt alone. I didn't know what to do. If he needed my heart, I would have given it to him. If he needed my left leg, I would have given it to him. If he needed my blood, I would have given it to him. It wasn't that easy though. He didn't need any of those things. I had to do something for him, but what. And then I heard another voice inside of me. What Dion wanted from me was for me to be his wife and share his life until death do us part. No one could give him that but me. Not the doctors. Not the nurses. Not his friends from school. Not even his family. So I at that moment, I made a decision that I knew Dion would be happy with. I found Robert, the chaplain. "Will you marry us? It's the only thing that I can think to do."

He looked at me for a slow moment and then said, "It would not be legally binding." I didn't care. I wasn't trying to get a court document. I just wanted to hold his hand and be pronounced his wife. Robert looked at me knowingly and I knew that he understood.

"This is a beautiful thing you're doing," he said. Then he told me that there would be a shift change in just a short time and he would ask the incoming Chaplain if he would perform the ceremony for me. He didn't think it would be a problem.

I felt a little better, more connected to Dion and more connected to God. I looked at the clock and wondered where Joy was. She should have been there by then. I prayed that nothing had happened to her. A few minutes later, she came through the door. I gave her a hug. She asked if I'd seen him. I told her that I had. I also told her that I wanted the Chaplain to marry us.

"That's wonderful," she exclaimed and hugged me again.

As Joy walked in, Dion's friends came up to meet her. Although I could see the pain and the fear in her eyes, she smiled at them graciously. I could also tell that she really appreciated them for being there.

Robert came over and I introduced Joy. He proceeded to introduce the new Chaplain. "This is John. He will be the Chaplain on call. Angela, I told him about your request," Robert said. I looked at the grandfatherly gentleman and suddenly I was comforted by his presence. John extended his hand and said kindly, "I'd be happy to marry you. Can we have prayer before we go back in to see Dion?"

We stood in the hallway between the two waiting rooms as John asked for God's mercy. After the prayer, John suggested that Joy take some time to see Dion before the marriage ceremony.

Joy and I walked back to the room where Dion was laid. She stood to his left side and looked at her son. She had tears in her eyes. I could see her struggling with the idea of "not my baby." She was telling him that she was there and that his father and brother loved him.

A few minutes passed as she whispered to him and then she took out her cell phone and called his big brother Tommy. She held the phone by Dion's ear as Tommy talked to his baby brother. I knew that had to be hard for him. Then she called Dion's father and again held the phone while his father spoke to him from a thousand miles away. Dion looked so helpless. I wondered what he was thinking. Was he scared? Was he even here?

I glanced down at the floor. Under the hospital bed, there were empty plastic cylinders that had once held blood. I counted them off in my head. Seven. That was how much blood they had given him.

For the first time, I noticed pools of blood under his bed, slowly spreading. The nurse had been right. The blood was leaking out even as they transfused more in.

The same two doctors approached us. They asked if we wanted to sit down. We walked behind the nurses' station where there were two chairs. One of the doctors looked so young. He didn't seem old enough to be saving anyone's life.

The doctors told us that Dion wasn't stabilizing. The accident had caused a lot of internal trauma that they could not repair. Machines were breathing for him and keeping his other functions working.

"Is he in pain?" Joy asked anxiously.

"He's heavily sedated," the young doctor told her. "But there is really nothing else we can do. The damage is just too severe. I'm sorry." His words penetrated the air, but not my ears or my heart. I was still hopeful that he would recover and we could have our happily ever after.

Joy walked away from me to call Dion's father. They spoke for a few minutes. When she came back, she said they had decided to take Dion off the respirator because they didn't want him to struggle to live. She assured me that it would be after the ceremony.

The chaplain came down the hallway and asked if we were ready. I looked at Joy and she nodded at me. I told him that we were ready.

We walked down the hall to Dion's room. There in that moment when I wanted more time, when I wanted to delay the truth, the world didn't slow down. There was no slow motion feeling, no stillness of time, just that moment rushing by way too quickly.

I took the Chaplain's hand and then proceeded to take Dion's in my own. His hand was still cold. I had hoped that my holding it would finally warm it up but to no avail. Joy touched Dion's head and held John's hand. We bowed our heads and then John began praying. I don't remember exactly what John said, however I do remember him saying "God has already joined Dion and Angela's hearts in marriage when he brought them together."

I thought, "Yes, he has."

When we finished, Joy and John left the room. I whispered in Dion's ear, "We's married now." And I smiled.

It wasn't the marriage ceremony I had dreamed of, but he was the man that I loved and I was the only one who could give him the one thing that I knew he really wanted. As I stood there looking at his face, I began to think back on the two weeks that had passed. I smiled. I even laughed a little. I was thinking about the visit to Gatorland and the fact that I'd converted him to oysters. I saw us sitting on the floor working on the scrapbook and eating guacamole in the big chair, me cooking dinner for him and us praying together. "We did have fun, huh, Dion," I whispered.

And then I felt the terror. All this was ending. My dream was only a dream. This man I loved, had fought for, was dying.

Not some time but at that time. That night I looked at his sweet face and my heart broke open. "Dion, I am so scared," I whispered to him. "I don't want to be in the room when you die. I'm sorry Dion. I just can't hear your last breath." I looked at him and then I looked out to where his mother was sitting.

She had her head down. I knew she was tired. I looked back at Dion and then I heard Joy call me. "Angela, maybe we should go to the waiting room for a while and just rest."

I nodded okay and rubbed Dion's hand and kissed his forehead. I walked over to Joy. She needed help with carrying some things. As we approached the ICU waiting room doors, a nurse called out to us, "Ladies, I think you ought to come back."

We dropped all of the stuff that we had in our hands and walked back with our arms around each other for support. At the door to his room the nurse spoke softly to us, "I guess he waited for you to walk away."

I turned to Joy and said, "That is just like him. He didn't want his two favorite women to be there when he died, so he waited until we walked away."

I remember standing to the right of Dion and looking at his face and thinking, "I can't believe that this is real. When am I going to wake up?"

John stood on the other side of the bed looking down at Dion. Then he looked at me and said, "It's okay to ask God questions, even Jesus had questions from the cross."

I looked up at John, "I have nothing to say to God." The conviction and bitterness in my voice surprised both of us.

A few moments later, as we walked out of the room the nurse said, "You two are very strong women." I didn't respond.

I didn't feel strong that night. I felt weak and hopeless. I couldn't begin to comprehend what had just happened. Joy and I walked back to the waiting room to get our stuff. From there we went downstairs to get the car. It was about 3 o'clock in the morning when we headed back to the apartment.

As we were driving back Joy asked about Dion having a dog. I told her that he did have a dog named Cujo. He didn't want to tell her because he knew that she would be upset that he was feeding a dog as well as trying to feed himself. She laughed a little bit as she remembered the love that Dion had for his dogs.

At the apartment, I took the potatoes out of the oven and put them in the fridge. I thought, "What a waste of food. I should have listened to that voice."

Joy was tired and ready to lie down. She went into the bedroom while I let Cujo out. Normally after being cooped up Cujo is anxious to play; however, this morning he knew something was different. He did his business and then walked back to the apartment on his own. I put him back in his kennel and then laid down on the bed with Joy. I wasn't sleepy and I figured that she wasn't either.

At one point I remember her closing her eyes. I was staring at the ceiling and then it was as if we switched places, I closed my eyes and she was looking up at the ceiling. I knew another day was coming, yet I was wondering how I could turn back time. I was hoping that Dion would come through the door. I knew that he wouldn't, but that didn't stop me from wanting it to happen.

Later that morning, I heard a knock on the door. It was Rick, one of Dion's friends. "Did I hear that Dion was in an accident?" he asked.

"Yes," I responded.

"Well, how is he?"

I looked at him wishing I could spare him the pain, but I couldn't. "He died this morning," I said carefully.

Rick slumped against the door. I helped him in and walked him into the den where he introduced himself to Joy. As I was about to sit down, my cell phone rang. It was my cousin. She asked the same question Rick had and I just caved in. I bolted into the bedroom that Dion and I had shared crying and gasping for breath. Joy was wise enough to leave me to cry alone.

It was midday when Dr. Miller and his wife arrived. I'd never met them before and I felt awkward. What do you say to the father of the man you loved when meeting him for the first time the day that his son died? Although they knew who I was, I still felt the I need to introduce myself. Who was I to these people now I wondered? I didn't have to be worried because they were very warm and caring.

When my mom arrived, everyone introduced themselves to each other. They were cordial and almost relaxed. Each was wearing their own mask of grief. This was not how it was supposed to be I thought to myself. After a while, we piled up in the PT Cruiser that Dr. Miller had rented from the airport.

Our first stop was at the Police Impound lot to retrieve Dion's belongings that he had with him at the time of the accident. We got his backpack and his helmet which was in a plastic bag and doused with blood. Next, we went to the hospital to pick up his cell phone. From there we went to a funeral home to make arrangements for his body to be shipped to New Jersey where the funeral would be held.

Joy, my mom and I decided to leave that night and drive back to Georgia. Joy's husband, Steve, was flying in that afternoon so as we were leaving Florida we picked him up and then headed north. Thank God for Steve's arrival because none of us we were in any shape to drive for an extended period of time.

My mom and I were sitting in the back seat. I dozed in and out of sleep. It was strange to be sitting in the back seat of my own car, but then again everything was strange at the time. As we rode along my thoughts went in and out of the present and the past. I thought about my mom's disdain for my relationship with Dion. She had called me every day for the first week to tell me how unhappy the family was. I had finally told her that if she didn't have something positive to say then she shouldn't call me. I didn't know why I even answered the phone when I saw her name. At one point, she had asked me if I was moving so fast because I was pregnant. Thank God I was in the mall parking lot when I got that call or I might have had an accident. I asked her if "hell no" would give her the answer she was looking for. Slowly my mind drifted back to the present and our journey.

We drove for about two hours. It was dark out and we were all exhausted so we decided to stop at a motel. We woke up the next morning and continued towards Georgia. We stopped for breakfast, but I didn't have much of an appetite.

After we started driving again, I leaned my head on the window and looked out into this field. I felt lost. I knew where I was going, I just didn't know why. At one point during the trip, I handed Joy a piece of paper saying that I wanted to speak at the funeral. When we stopped at a rest area, I got out to stretch. Joy told me that if I didn't feel like speaking at the funeral, I could write something down and put it in the program. "I want to speak," I told her insistently.

As we continued our trip, I thought about the drive south to Florida just a few weeks earlier with Dion. The anticipation of a new life together had made the whole world sparkle. That day the world was grey and flat.

When we got to Joy's house, we were greeted by Tommy, Dion's grandmother, and Hausan, Dion's cousin. We went upstairs to the room that would have been mine and Dion's. There was a lot of crying and hugging. I went over to Tommy. I didn't know what to say to him. I knew that whatever I said would not help or make him feel better. So, I told him that I loved his brother very much. Tommy looked at me intently and then looked away and said, "My brother would have gone to hell if it were not for you." I gave Tommy a hug and we cried together.

Before we left, Joy gave me the wedding band Dion had purchased for our wedding day. She was holding back the tears as she handed me the box. She told me that Dion loved me very much. I could tell that she was sad for me and the fact that I did not get the wedding that I wanted. "I am grateful to you for loving my Dion so much." She told me, "You are my hero." There was no more holding back the tears at that point for either of us.

After a while, my mom and I continued on the road to Nashville, Tennessee. While we were traveling she told me that she was glad I was a woman of my convictions. "Why," I wondered, "had she not appreciated my steadfastness before this unfortunate tragedy?" I didn't talk much to my mom on the ride home. I remember her saying that this experience would change me. I wondered if she couldn't see that it already had. Talking to her about Dion was a sensitive subject before and I knew that now it was going to be an even trickier.

As the landscape streamed by my window, I withdrew into myself. The events of the last few weeks floated around my consciousness like debris from a shipwreck. Some moments I recognized. Some pieces seemed like strangers. I thought about the night before Dion died and the petty argument we had. I'd assumed that we would eventually kiss and make up like we always had. I figured he would come home from school and all would be well. I was wrong. Everything felt wrong. Like the time he had left me for ten months and now he'd done it again. Left me. Permanently. I was again alone, again crying. Not hating him again. Wanting to see him again. Not understanding why again. Missing him again. Loving him again. Wishing he would somehow come back to me. The only thing that I was not doing this time that I had done the last time he left me was praying. I had no reason to talk to God.

I thought about the voice I'd heard. No need to make dinner. What had that been? If God were sending me a message why not send something useful. Stay home today. Love each other. Why not save Dion? What was the purpose he and I should have had?

The voices added up to no more than the fairytales I'd read as a child. The prince was gone and with him the happy ending. On God's advice I'd opened my heart. Believed in a purpose and had been crushed. If this were the nature of God, then I had no more use for Him.

In this grief, even breathing hurt. I missed Dion. I missed the feeling that life and even love made some kind of sense. The thought occurred to me that if Dion could not be with me here, then I could go to him.

Journal Entry

If I live to see next year at this time, I wonder how I will be because right now I hate the sight of each day. Each day reminds me that there will never be another day that I will see Dion. Each day I get further and further away from the last time I kissed Dion. Each day is a reminder of how empty and lost I feel because I'm no longer with Dion. Each day sucks.

I'm not happy. I'm not okay. I don't feel strong. I truly feel as though death is the only cure for my pain. I'm unsure where to go or what to do with myself. Anger is beginning to rise up inside me. I feel all alone. No one knows my pain but me. I miss my Dion.

CHAPTER SEVENTEEN

The Sun Was Shining Brightly

A month before the accident, before the world had ended, Dion's mom had invited us to go to North Carolina for a family vacation. She had rented a beach house for a week. Dion had declined because he couldn't miss more than two days of school. After his passing, Joy asked again if I wanted to go along with them. I decided to go because I knew that he would have really wanted to be with his family.

I flew to Wilmington, North Carolina a few days late, wanting the family to have some private time. The sun had set when I landed at the airport. By the time I got to the house most of the people were already asleep. I went into the room they prepared for me and began to listen to CDs that Dion had made for our wedding. I'd not heard the song that he had chosen to be our wedding song. I didn't know which CD he had put it on and I wanted to hear it. I asked Dion as if he were there with me to please let me hear the song that night. A short time later, as I was writing in my journal, a song began to play. I knew that it must be the song he had chosen. And I began to cry. The song was *Never Felt This Way* by Brian McKnight.

> *"When I look into your eyes*
> *Then I realize*
> *That all I need is you in my life.*
> *All I need is you in my life.*
> *'Cuz I've never felt this way about lovin'..."*

The lyrics perfectly described how we had felt a month ago. Listening to them now, I felt like my heart might explode. We had come so far, through so many arguments and across our past histories littered with betrayals and disappointment to really find love. And now that love, all that I needed and truly wanted in my life, had been taken away. I turned the music off and cried myself to sleep.

The next day, with my mask firmly in place, I met some of the family that I'd not met before. One of whom was Tyler, Dion's little brother. He was quiet and I was not sure if he liked me. Not that I was likable at that time.

That evening I got a text message from my friend, Nikiah, congratulating me on my engagement. I decided to call her back to tell her the bad news. Upon hearing the news, she was devastated and stammered an apology. While I was on the phone with her, Tommy came up stairs to ask me to come down and chill with his family. I decided to take him up on his offer but not until I finished my conversation with Nikiah. I spoke with her for a few more minutes and then went down stairs to hang out. I was happy that they wanted to include me and wondered how long they were going to see me as a part of their family.

The next morning we got on the road for New Jersey. At one point I forgot where we were going. Why was I going to New Jersey? Then I remembered we were going for a funeral...to bury Dion. It still didn't make sense to me. It just didn't seem real. My mind wasn't registering the reality of his death let alone his burial.

Upon our arrival, I met more family members as we prepared for the funeral. It was overwhelming to be meeting all of those people and dealing with the reality of the funeral. So much so that I decided I didn't want to speak at the funeral.

Instead of speaking, I would just to do an insert. I typed up a note that I'd written to Dion a few months ago and put it on the back of a picture of the two of us. It was my love letter to him.

Dion,

I have never felt this way about love and

I love how I am feeling. I love you and appreciate you for being in my life.

You are so beautiful.

I love that you love me. We have been together since 2003 and I cannot imagine what my life would have been like without you in it. You said that I changed you, but the truth is that we changed each other for the better. I know that we have a love that is like no other.

People wish for the kind of love that we share and they may never find it. I thank God that we found each other. You are my teddy bear, my love bug, my sweetheart and so much more.

I will love you always and forever.

Your Baby, your Angel, your princess, your Angela

That evening, Joy, Dr. Miller and I went to the funeral home for an open viewing of the body. I'd bought Dion a grey suit to be buried in. Joy had given me a wedding band to put with him in the casket. I'd had the ring engraved with the simple words, "Love Always."

I was numb. I found myself in disbelief and denial as I approached the casket. Even as I looked at his body lying there, I just did not feel that he was gone. He looked like Dion. I reached into the casket and to put the wedding band on his finger. I couldn't get it on so I simply placed it on his body. It was at that moment that I knew he was no longer there. His hand was cold and stiff. His body was lifeless like a mannequin. It was clear to me now that the real Dion no longer existed.

I slowly felt the tears gathering in my eyes and then I just couldn't help it. I cried. I loved him and I missed him and I knew that I would never see him again. It hurt my heart, my mind, my spirit. I didn't want to understand the pain. I just wanted this tragedy of a broken heart to go away. I wanted Dion back.

Unexpectedly, Dr. Miller put his arm around me. I don't remember if he said anything, but I appreciated him wanting to comfort me. It still seemed strange to me…my interaction with Dion's father. I didn't expect him to be so caring having raised all boys. And from what I'd heard from Dion, he was extremely hard and strict. But I liked and welcomed his caring and his comfort especially in the absence of my parents.

That night my parents, brother, aunt, and friend arrived. I stayed with them that night at their hotel knowing that the funeral was the next day. That morning as I was getting ready for the funeral, I looked at myself in the mirror. I had to hold back the tears. Why was I getting all dressed up to go to the funeral of the man that I was supposed to be spending the rest of my life with? I had no answers but a million questions ran through my mind. As I put on my makeup and prepared to leave I found myself grateful that at least my family was there to support me.

We left the hotel and went to meet Dion's family at Dr. Miller's house. I got in the car with Joy and her husband, Steve as we headed to the church. When we got to the church I was surprised that there were so many people attending. Members of my extended family had come from Detroit, Chicago, and New York City. I looked down the steps and saw that one of my friends, Linara had shown up with my roommates from NYU. When I saw them, I lost it. I felt so overwhelmed. I hadn't realized that they loved me enough to show their support in that way.

I sat with the family on the front row. At one point, there was a slide show of pictures of Dion and me as well as of him and his family. My cousin Bonita sang "His Eye is On the Sparrow." Joy stood up to give remarks. She wore a black and white outfit to the funeral. She stated that she wore those colors to symbolize her mourning his death with the black and celebrating his life with the white. Listening to how eloquent and composed she was, I was in awe because I knew I was in no shape to speak. I was glad that I'd put my thoughts and prayers as an insert in the program.

After the funeral, we caravanned to the cemetery. Outside it was a beautiful summer day. The sun was shining brightly, but inside my heart I felt a growing darkness.

I wore all black. I looked to find a silver lining in this. I grasped at something I had heard - that if on the day of the funeral the sun is shining then the deceased is happy to be at rest. If it is raining on the day of the funeral, then the deceased wasn't ready to leave. The sun was out. Dion must have been ready to go, but that thought did not give me any peace.

Each of the mourners were given a flower as they approached the gravesite. There were four chairs sitting beside the casket. In each of the four chairs a single rose had been placed. I was standing behind the chairs. I didn't realize that one of the seats was for me. Joy wanted to make sure that I sat down and got a rose for myself. She leaned over and whispered in my ear that the roses were a symbol of how much Dion loved to give me roses.

I don't remember most of what the minister said at the gravesite. However, I do remember him directing us to place each of our roses on the casket. As I walked toward Dion's casket, which was suspended over his grave, I couldn't believe that this was my life. I should have been holding a bouquet of roses and placing a ring on his hand. With each step that I took toward the casket I thought about flowers blooming to die, and how each of us are nurtured to grow and spread our own unique beauty; yet, eventually we will all die and return to the Creator. Dion's return to the Creator was the same as the flowers that had been placed on his casket.

When we got back to the church, I sat with my friends. We ate and we laughed, although my laughter was strained. The stories and memories being shared fell short of Dion being there; however, I loved having the support of my friends and family. Given that Father's Day was approaching, I gave Dr. Miller a father's day card after the funeral. I wanted to thank him for creating Dion and subsequently, creating love in my life.

I also sent God a note. As the numbness wore off, a righteous anger rose in its place.

"Why me?" The note started. It had taken me some time to get up the courage to write those words because I knew what God's response would be. "Why not you?" I did not want to hear that. I did not want to hear anything except Dion's voice. I did not want to feel anything except Dion's kiss. I did not want anything except to have Dion's arms wrapped around me telling me that it was going to be alright.

I took his death as a form of punishment. I wondered if I had offended God in some way. Did he take Dion away from me to teach me a lesson? I started talking to God, but I am not sure that what I was saying could be considered prayer. I was conversing with God by lashing out in anger and hurt and pain.

Why would a caring God take the man I loved? And I wasn't sure that I wanted to live on this earth without Dion.

Journal Entry

I am so sorry for whatever I did. I'm so sorry I can't live with this thing. I don't feel strong anymore. I know that everything happens for a reason, but I don't know why this had to happen.

"*And yet, I suppose you mourn the loss or the death of what you thought your life was, even if you find your life is better after. You mourn the future that you thought you'd planned.*"

-Lynn Redgrave

CHAPTER EIGHTEEN

"Better"

The next morning, I told my family goodbye and got in the car with Linara and my NYU roommates. I was riding back to New York to get a few last things from my apartment and to see Linara's father who had been diagnosed with lung cancer and was not expected to live much longer.

It felt strange to be going back to this city where I had spent most of my nights on the phone with Dion. When we arrived at the apartment, I went into my bedroom. I started trying to figure out what I was going to take with me. I looked at my phone and thought, "Dion will be calling me any minute now." I stopped myself. I said to myself, "Angela, get it together. He won't ever call you again."

Fortunately, I'd saved his answering machine messages and his voice was recorded in the Build-A-Bear that he had made me. Each time I pushed the right hand of the bear I heard Dion's voice say, "Baby, congratulations I love you." I did not realize it before, but his voice sounded far away. In some small way, I was able to carry a piece of Dion with me no matter where I was which was important to me because lately I had been doing a lot of traveling. Now I was getting ready to travel from New York back to my home state of Tennessee.

On the flight back to Tennessee, I had a two hour layover in Charlotte. I went to the gate looking for a place to sit that wasn't too close to anybody else. I saw a set of three empty

119

chairs. I could sit in the middle and have a seat to separate me from the men that were on either side.

I sat there fidgeting because I get impatient when it comes to waiting in airports. After a few minutes, a woman sat down to my right. I don't remember how we started talking but I remember her eyes matched the green in her jacket.

She asked me if I was traveling for business or pleasure. I was unsure of how to answer her, "I'm not sure that I fit in either category. I've just buried my husband."

Her eyes softened, "I'm sorry to hear that. It must be hard for you."

I nodded my head, afraid to speak.

She filled in the empty space, "I lost my daughter when she was just ten days old."

I told her that I was sorry to hear that. I showed her a picture of Dion and me.

She studied the picture and then smiled at me, "You can see that he's in love with you."

"We were in love with each other," I told her.

And that started our conversation. Her baby had died ten years ago, but she thought of her every day. She didn't try to make it better for me. She wasn't a tourist on this painful journey gazing in from the outside. She had her own loss and didn't try to take mine from me.

The gate agent announced that our flight was boarding. I had hoped to sit next to her but no such luck. When we landed, she gave me her card and told me to call her for lunch sometime.

Even though I didn't want to be in Nashville back at my parents' house, I knew I didn't have anywhere else to go. I woke up every morning wondering why I was still alive and why was I still in Nashville. How was it that I still knew how to breathe? Why was I not waking up beside Dion? Question after question invaded my thoughts and my mind. I didn't like the reality of the answers.

It was hard for me to function. My mind was on Dion constantly. Everything reminded me of him. Everywhere I went I wished that Dion was there. Regardless of who else was there, I really just wanted him. So my sadness and my journaling became my everyday solace.

Journal Entry

Every time I go somewhere I wish that you were right there with me. Every day when I wake up, moving in my reality is hard. No date passes without my wishing and wanting you. Each night falls with my feeling confused. Why I'm no longer falling asleep in your arms.

I feel alone and unsettled. I'm unsure of where to go or what to do. I still can't believe my fairy tale is over. Sadness has fallen over me. No longer do I feel anything except the torture of living on this earth without you. I loved him for so long that I didn't really remember what it was like not to love him. He was a part of my world, my daily routine, my diet, my ritual, he was and will always be a part of me.

My friends didn't get it, and I learned not to expect that from them. My family didn't get it either. I was hurting. The pain was constant. Most of the things I did, I did so that they would feel okay with my sadness. If I could not take away my own pain, maybe I could lessen their sorrow but I didn't care about anything and I wasn't sure if I ever would again. During that time my friend Marsha would call or text me daily to make sure that I was okay. She may not have always gotten it or understood, but she felt an overwhelming need to check on me daily without trying to make me "get over" my sadness.

Talking to Joy was comforting; however, it was also hard sometimes. I knew that we had to be there for each other. Somehow, I had it in my mind that I had to grieve for everyone else. I grieved for a mother losing her son, for a big brother losing a baby brother, and for children losing an uncle. I grieved for the people that I felt didn't understand why I was grieving, my parents, my brother, my family, and my friends. Somehow I thought that if I took my mind off of myself that maybe it would be easier than grieving for myself.

I've never been afraid of death and at that point in my life I was less afraid than ever. I felt ready to die. I thought about all of my wonderful experiences…my relationships, my travels, my exposure to education and various cultures. I'd lived a full life. I had people that loved me and that I loved. Life couldn't get any fuller than that could it? So I was ready to live with Dion in heaven instead I wrote to him.

> *I woke up this morning with a lump in my throat. The thought of not being with Dion makes me sick. I'm still in disbelief about this. I miss him so much. I can't believe that it has almost been a month since the accident. It still feels like yesterday even though we've been through all the ceremonies. Your mom's friend Emily told me something that made me happy yet sad. She said that you will find a mate for me, but if I am not accepting of him it will break your heart. You really want me to be happy? I wish I didn't have to go through this. I just wanted to be with you. Your mom would have been the best mother-in-law. I wanted to share all of our moments together not with some man*

that you will now choose for me. I know that you are happy in heaven. As much as I would like to experience love again, I really just wish I could be with you.

I have decided to get a tattoo. I am excited about getting my tattoo. I'm going to get a teddy bear holding a rose.

I hope that when I get to heaven we will reunite and laugh together. I never was afraid to die Dion, but I'm afraid that I will be here a little while longer and therefore I will be older than you. I wish that you would come back to me. Most of the time the couples that I see make me sad or even jealous. I hate this feeling. This is the worst kind of broken heart.

I asked myself about this brokenhearted Angela. Who was she? She didn't seem like much to me. She just wanted to get this life over with. So many people tried to encourage me. Some went about it in a manner that was loving and others went about it in a manner that would simply and absolutely piss me off.

I don't know how many times people tried to comfort me with a variation of "When God takes something away from you, he gives you something better." The word "better" became my arch enemy. I didn't want to hear that word. Ever! Especially not to describe how my life was going to be after the man I loved had just died.

What those words conveyed to me was, "Now that he is gone and out of the way you can get something better." The audacity of the thought led me to consider other similar questions. Would people who have lost their parents or children somehow get better parents or better children? No!

I think that JonBenét Ramsey's mother phrased it best. People would say to her, "She is in a better place." Mrs. Ramsey would reply, "Not that I think I'm bigger or better than God, but I would like to think that my arms were the best place." These were my sentiments exactly.

My grief did not keep me from sleep. In fact, most nights I looked forward to going to bed. Some nights I would cry myself to sleep, other nights I would just drop off into a void. Every night I would hope to see Dion in my dreams. I looked forward to snuggling under my covers and dozing off so that I could hug and kiss him and be with him until I woke up.

Journal Entry

Thank you for coming to see me in my dream. You were sitting on the floor and I was sitting on the bed. You were playing peek-a-boo with me. There were no words. I finally got down on the floor and gave you a big hug. I knew you are visiting me. You had both of your legs. I said, thank you for coming to see me. I told you that I missed you. You looked at me with a smile and if I remember correctly you said "I know." I can't remember if you said I miss you too or love you too. Something you said made me look at you and smile and think this is more than a dream. He really is here.

The dreams went on for a while and after a few weeks at home, I knew that I didn't want to stay in Tennessee. I wanted to get away from all of the pain, hoping, and wishing so I started to look for jobs in other states. Plus, I didn't want my Master's degree to go to waste. I wasn't sure that I wanted to go back to Atlanta with all of the bittersweet memories, even though Joy offered me a room in her home. New York City was too expensive. I thought about Chicago. We had family and friends in Chicago. They might know of some jobs available. I made a few phone calls and sent out emails.

In July, I heard from my aunt whose brother lived in Chicago. He told her that he was opening another elementary school and they were in need of a Dean of Students.

I sent an email with my resume to the school. They contacted me and conducted a phone interview. A few days later they called to say that I had the job. I told everyone the good news. I moved to Chicago at the end of July. I liked being in a new place and I knew that I was about to learn so many different things. I actually felt a little optimistic.

As a part of a counseling group I had participated in prior to moving, I'd been reading *Recovering from the Losses in Life* by W. H. Wright. I identified with the chapter that discussed how we don't recognize every loss in our life and grieve for it individually. As a result, it is hard when we deal with a huge loss like that of a loved one.

There were questions in the back of the book that related to the material from each chapter. One of the questions was, 'Do you cry every time you think of the person or hear the person's name?" My initial response was no. I was proud of myself. I figured that meant that I was handling my grief well. "Chicago is the place I will pull my life back together," I told myself naively.

Normally, I have a good sense of direction. I can find my way around pretty easily, but the streets of Chicago threw me. I got lost on an almost daily basis. Even traveling over what should have been familiar terrain, the route from my house to the school evaded me. It was incredibly frustrating because I felt like a stranger every day. I wrote it off to being in a new city and working a new job but it unsettled me to no end. Little did I realize that this experience was a sign of grief.

I liked the school and the staff. I was adjusting to the responsibilities of my new job just fine until I had to confront a young boy who was disrupting class by throwing tantrums as well as chairs and pencils and whatever else he could make fly. That day while driving from work, I had the sudden impulse to call my mom. When she answered, I was crying which was not something that I wanted her to know that I did, especially when I wasn't sure why I was crying. The incident with the child had not been that big a deal.

"I think I should come get you," she told me.

That wasn't what I wanted. I just wanted to calm down, but I had no idea how to do that. By the time, I got off the phone, I thought that I had pulled myself together. I was due at the principal's office at our sister school to give a report on the unruly student. On the way, I ran into a fellow teacher. She took one look at me and asked, "How are you doing?

Before I could answer, I was crying again. The tears ran down my cheeks and all I could do was shake my head. I found the courage to tell her about Dion. She gave me a hug. I wiped away the tears and went into the principal's office. She asked how my meeting with the student had gone. As I was telling her, she leaned in closer and held up her hand to hush me. "How are *you* doing?" she asked. Down came the waterfall again. She came around her desk to my side. "What's going on?" she asked.

My story came tumbling out including how I thought I'd been dealing with the loss of Dion, but I really had not been able to. Even though I told her that I didn't want to leave my job, she thought that it would be better for me to take care of myself and resign from my position. She set up an appointment for me to talk to the social worker from her school that evening.

We met at a quiet restaurant. She had been helping me get acclimated to my job, so I felt comfortable talking to her. I told her that I made a commitment to this job and I didn't just want to leave it.

She nodded her understanding and said, "Sometimes taking a step down is taking a step up. Knowing that you need to take care of yourself is where you find the victory not in pushing yourself to do something that you may not be ready for."

She also told me that I was like a cake, full of all the ingredients that made me whole and good all by myself. Dion had been the icing. He was added on to what was already cake. He didn't make me better but he added to what was already good. Before him I was cake and after him I would still be cake.

I finally broke down and realized that no matter what I did or where I did it, I would not be happy. I came to the realization that no matter where I went I couldn't run from myself or my grief. Not that I really expect to be happy, but I was so irritable and frustrated. I hated my life. I wished that there was no tomorrow for me. Life sucked at that time.

I resigned and moved in with Jewell a friend of mine from my home church who now lived in Chicago. She was working on her doctorate in social work. I called her Jewelry Box because she was like a treasure to me. She had a wonderful spirit and was so full of insight. My first night there, we sat on the couch and she asked me to tell her about Dion.

I did not hesitate to dive into my memories. We sat for hours with me doing most of the talking. She would ask a few questions that would rekindle other memories and I would tell those stories. She had tears in her eyes as I finished. She told me that it was great story and she could see it being a book one day. And then she asked me what I figured everyone was afraid to ask me but were probably wondering, "Have you ever thought about committing suicide?"

I told her that I had thought about suicide because I wanted to see Dion again. However, I knew that Dion would not want me to kill myself. Would he want me to miss him? Yes. Would he want me to mourn his loss? Yes. But the one thing that he would also want for me was to be happy. I could still hear his voice clearly in my heart, "Angela, I just want you to be happy."

I was relieved that Jewelry Box had asked me that question. I wanted someone to know the full depth of my pain and how far I might go to escape that pain. Most people who contemplate suicide or who have suicidal thoughts don't want to die, they really just want someone to know how much pain they are feeling.

JB encouraged me to tell my story and to let people know that I was mad at God and that it was okay to get mad at God. She helped me to understand that being mad at God does not stop Him from loving you and that your being mad at him doesn't mean that you don't love him. It may, in fact, deepen your relationship with him.

Even though I wasn't talking to God I was talking to Dion. We still had a connection.

Dion, I miss you baby very much. I wish I could call you and hear your loving voice. I just want to tell you about everything that I have been experiencing but I guess you can see it. Wherever I end up, I know that I will need to be in some type of group or individual counseling. It was a good day yesterday but I still miss you like crazy. I'm still in shock that you are not here to share this with me in the physical sense.

CHAPTER NINETEEN

Good Grief

A week later my mom showed up to move me back home to Tennessee. I wasn't happy about it, but then again I wasn't happy about anything. I wasn't sure what I would do. I didn't feel motivated to do much. My mind and heart spent hours each day among my memories of Dion. I did know that I needed grief counseling so I called a few counseling centers to see what type of services they provided. None of them had what I needed.

A minister from my church suggested Alive Hospice. A week later, I began grief counseling there with a woman named Nicole. I loved being able to talk to someone who was objective. She didn't know me and she hadn't known Dion. She just listened.

I told her the chronology of my recent life events from graduating to moving to Florida to getting engaged to my fiancé dying. I could see compassion on her face. "Wow," she said to me mid-way through our first session, "just about everyone goes through each of those life changes but over time. You went through them all within a single month. The dust hadn't had time to settle on one event before the next came rolling in."

She compared me to a beautiful vase that had been shattered and even though glue and patience could put the vase back together again it would never be quite the same. What happened to me had shaken and shattered my being. I was broken...broken hearted and this experience was going to change me forever. I was so pleased that she got it. I was sad and I was changed. The word 'better' never crossed her lips.

She told me that the frustration that I felt while I was in Chicago regarding feeling lost and not having a good sense of direction had to do with my grieving. Everything that I was feeling was grief. I didn't want to talk to my friends about their problems because I didn't believe that they really had anything to be sad or worried about. I didn't believe that the couples who I saw were really in love. I didn't believe that anyone loved their boyfriend or girlfriend; husband or wife as much as Dion and I had loved each other.

I slowly realized that I was not going to get through this grief on my own or with mere human help. I knew that I needed to go to God for help. I knew that he was the only one who could truly get me through this. This task was not easy. I was still mad and wondered if I had failed his test. I began by turning to the book I had relied on before Dion's passing.

Journal Entry

I bought a new Bible yesterday and inscribed in it "to Angela A. Grant in my season of expectancy." I started reading it again last night. I had devotional time. I also bought a new journal that focuses on the fruits of the spirit and a book of daily meditations for healing after loss. I was reading one today and it brought tears to my eyes. "It is the person, after all, whom we want, not the grief."

CHAPTER TWENTY

You Can Quote Me on That

A friend of mine gave me a Maya Angelou Hallmark card. You can often times tell when someone has spent time looking for just the right card. This was one of those cards. Angelou's poem, "Continue" was the message in the card.

> *"I don't know if I can continue, even today, always liking myself. But what I learned to do many years ago was to forgive myself. It is very important for every human being to forgive herself or himself because if you live, you will make mistakes- it is inevitable...The real difficulty is to overcome how you think about yourself. If we don't have that we never grow, we never learn, and sure as hell we should never teach."*

I put the card on my dresser so that I would see it every morning and read the word 'continue'. There was power in that word for me. I had to keep going and pushing and pressing and seeking and learning.

I began to think of the many different people in my life and how much they had made an impact on me whether they knew it or not. What was I going to do, stop loving the people that had loved me? Not likely. I started thinking about the different things that I do that are hard, but I do them because I want to show my friends and family that I love and support them. Things like going to graduations, weddings, birthdays, funerals and making hospital visits.

Instead of waiting for people to do something for me to make me feel good, I decided that I wanted to do something for other people. I have always loved quotes so I decided to put an inspirational quote a week on my voicemail.

I looked in my quote book to find the most meaningful quote that expressed what I was going through that day. I wanted to let people know that it was okay to hurt. However, it was not okay to simply remain a victim of the hurt; instead, they had to learn and grow from it. I looked through the pages until I found the perfect quote attributed to George C. Wolfe. "I can't live in yesterday's pain, I can't live without it." The quote was perfect enough and he was even a graduate from NYU just like me!

Over the next few days, people who called me, left messages saying how much they liked the quote and how powerful it was. It was working!

A few days later, I was visiting a friend of mine when my phone rang. I saw that it was my cousin BJ. I let it ring through to my voicemail rather than be rude to my friend. It occurred to me that she might not like my message. Leaving my friend's house, I listened to my cousin's message. She got right to her opinion, "take that quote off your cell, it sounds terrible."

I didn't want to hear any more of her animosity towards my voicemail quote, but I decided to call her back anyway. The conversation went well for about thirty seconds and then she said, "Angela, what is that message. That is depressing, that doesn't sound good, you need to change that. "

"I like that quote. It's uplifting to me." I told her politely.

She put in her two cents again, "Uplifting. Unh-uh. That is sad and it doesn't sound good."

I could feel the anger in me rising. Not just about this quote issue but about a collection of issues going back years. She kept criticizing me and suddenly I just wanted her to shut up and get it through her head that the quote wasn't changing just because she didn't like it. She kept pushing her 'I hate the quote' agenda until I lost it.

"I don't give a F_ _ _ what you think. If I want to leave a quote on my voicemail, then I will do just that. I don't care what you think!" The words just came rolling out of me.

Complete dead silence. I didn't know if she had hung up or not, but I clicked off. I was shaking. Why didn't she understand that I was hurting and that I was sensitive and if I tried to say in a nice way initially that the quote wasn't going to change, then why not just drop it?

At first I saw my outburst as a setback in my climb toward peace and forgiveness. However, Nicole had another thought. She suggested, "It might be,", "You are reclaiming your life. Stepping back in an authentic way, stronger than ever before."

November rolled around bringing Dion's birthday. Even though I didn't have a specific idea, .I wanted to do something to acknowledge the day. I was going to New York City that weekend and I asked Nicole for a suggestion. She told me that people release balloons on occasions like that; however, all I could think of was a bird choking on a balloon. I didn't want to do that.

She didn't venture another guess, she just told me, "You're good at knowing what is right for you. I know you will figure something out."

I woke up the next morning with a poem in my heart. It was a birthday poem for Dion. I went into the office in my cousin's Brooklyn apartment and found some paper. I began to write:

I believe in yesterday for yesterday was what I knew.

Even though yesterday wasn't your Birthday, but it was the birth f something new.

No not new like in a gift or present, but rather something new in me.

You opened up my heart and made me see love differently.

Discovering the part of you and the heart f you that I knew all along was there.

You opened up that part of me that was content with "I don't care."

When I asked God to send me a man that could challenge me of course I didn't know what he was going to do.

So in all of my asking God knew exactly who to choose.

He chose for me a life size teddy bear with "bad boy" issues, who was originally from the north so he rocked Timberland shoes.

He chose for me a smile that could part a cloudy day. A heart that chipped away at my heart and tore down the sign that said "stay away."

He sent me a kiss that would always ease the pain and a hug that would protect me from tornado, avalanche or hurricane.

He sent me a man that reminded me of myself.

He sent me a soul mate when I felt I was losing my own soul.

He sent me a friend who turned out to be the best gift I'd ever get.

I asked for him in 2002. I received him in 2003. He disappeared in 2003. He returned in 2004. He proposed in 2004. I said "yes" in 2004. We laughed and cried in 2005. We fell deeper in love in 2006. We got engaged in 2006. I married him in 2006. He died in 2006. I cried in 2006.

Little did I know that I loved him all of my life, cause we were meant to be.

No matter how long we are apart I will always remember the birth you gave to me.

Happy Birthday Dion

I also wrote a blog on my MySpace page:

Today would have been his 27th birthday. I would have cooked him a cake and I would have taken him out to dinner. I would have sent him happy birthday text messages and voicemails. I would be singing him Happy Birthday out loud instead of in my heart. I would be hugging and kissing him and telling him how much I love him. I would be thanking God for another day on this earth with him. Now I'm left with the memories and thanking God for the time we did get to share.

Although I'm not crying right now, my heart is hurting and wanting and waiting. He was my husband he was my best friend. He was the love that I never knew was in search for me. He was and is the mate of my soul. He gave me a lesson in love that I will always have with me until I breathe my last breath.

I will always love him. Happy Birthday Angel!

CHAPTER TWENTY-ONE

Do You Think…?

My cousin Charys' fiancé Rob was throwing her a surprise party in Washington, DC. I wasn't sure that I wanted to go. I didn't want to be the sad, grieving girl at the party; however, Rob would not take "no" for an answer. He said it would mean a lot to Charys if I were there.

Even though that may have been true, I also knew that it was not just my sorrow that held me back. The truth of the matter was I felt a tinge of jealousy. My cousin had her fiancé. He was doing things for her and all was well in their world. I wasn't happy with myself for feeling that way so I made a conscious decision to get over myself and to go and be happy for my cousin.

Rob picked me and two of Charys' other friends up from the airport. When we got to the house, Charys saw us. We yelled surprise when we saw her and she began to cry. I knew that I had made the right decision.

The next night on the way to a restaurant, Rob was driving just the two of us in his car. Charys and her other friends were in another car behind us. Rob asked me, "So how are you doing?"

I took a moment before I answered appreciating his sincerity in asking me that question. "I have my moments. Sometimes I am okay and other times I am not so okay."

"Do you think that you will ever love again or want to get married again?

It wasn't the first time that someone had asked me that. I had never answered the question before. I had just changed the subject; yet, this time an answer came out. "Yeah, I will love again." I'm not sure that I really believed what I was saying. Part of me felt like "yes" was the answer that would make him feel okay or feel like I was okay.

Later that night, a new thought occurred to me. Not to love anymore would be to kill Dion all over again. I realized that Dion had taught me a great lesson in love and not just in intimate relationships. I had learned that love is to be given fully in all relationships. As I contemplated the future, I thought to myself, "Whether or not I find 'Mr. Right,' I still have love to share." Yet, I realized that I had to start with loving myself.

I remember doing an experiment once in college with a mirror. Each of us was told to look into our reflection and then write down what we saw. My first notes were about my physical features; however, as I focused on my eyes I started writing about my life experiences.

After Dion died I didn't like looking in the mirror. I would only look long enough to comb my hair or to put in my contacts but not long enough to look into my eyes. I was afraid of what I might actually see. And then came the day when I looked and didn't look away. I was ready to face me again, for better or worse, if only because Dion would want me to.

I looked at her; I could see that she had a glimmer of hope in her right eye and the pain of her history in the left eye. She didn't notice me watching, but she knew that I was there. I saw a tear building up on her eyelid, then it dropped down to the tip of her eyelash it lingered there for only a moment as morning dew on a rose petal. The tear rolled down her cheek on to her lip and she closed her eyes. She tasted the saltiness of the tear. She was filled with sorrow.

"There is a great difference between knowing and understanding: you can know a lot about something and not really understand it."

-*Charles Kettering*

CHAPTER TWENTY-TWO

A New Understanding

Tension between my parents and I, actually between me and most of my family, was still running pretty high. I didn't know how to express my sorrow and they had given up directly approaching me and were simply giving me space. I felt like a ghost in a way. No one could really touch me. I couldn't feel much except anger at not being able to reclaim the life I had lost. I was holding onto the anger, keeping it between me and my loss. If my anger were big enough, there was no room for sorrow.

Through my sessions with Nicole I realized that I had been feeling that the only way to show my father how much I was hurting was to hate him and my mother...forever. Nicole helped me see that hating them would not bring Dion back nor would it make me feel any better. I knew that Dion would not want me to hold a grudge against anyone let alone my parents.

The next week I was riding in my father's car. I looked over at him and said, "I need to tell you something."

He nodded for me to go ahead.

"I was so hurt by the way you acted towards my wanting to live with Dion that I had planned on hating you forever, but then I realized that Dion would not want that and it would take more energy to hate you than to love you and hating you forever will never bring Dion back."

I expected to see some remorse in his eyes, some tinge of his own pain; nevertheless, my father showed little emotion. He told me that as a parent he did not have a problem with Dion and me marrying, yet he did not like the fact that we were moving in with each other before marriage. He and my mother did not feel that I had had enough "life" experience.

I informed my father that I did have a few relationships in college but none that lasted long enough for me to want to write home. It was not that I did not have "life" experience it was that I did not wish to share my "life" experiences with my parents.

He still thought that living together before marriage was wrong and wouldn't budge. Hell, I thought it was too; however, I decided to follow my heart and not my values at the time. I'm not sure what I wanted or expected from him, but I definitely wanted more than I got from the exchange. Oh well, it was a start.

When Thanksgiving came, I was nervous to be around my family. My uncle, Jones, always liked people to get up after Thanksgiving dinner and either express what they were thankful for or to perform some type of God-given talent. Some people sang, others did a monologue, and still others told a story. I wasn't sure that I wanted to do anything but I knew that I wanted Dion to be known. I wanted my family to know that I did love him.

When it was my turn, I stood behind the couch. I felt the tears pushing through and even though I didn't feel comfortable crying in front of my family, I went ahead. I showed them a picture book of me and Dion so that those who had never met him could see how happy I was when I was with him.

I told them about how we had met. I told them that I would give anything for one more day to hold him and to make sure he knew, in his bones, how solid and endless my love was for him. I left them with this, "I used to like the saying that everything happens for a reason, but in this case I don't know why it happened. When people say that to me now, 'there is a reason for this loss,' it stings. I can only reply that this happened so that I may find purpose in my pain."

My mom was surprised that I spoke at all. A friend of hers who was visiting stared at me the whole time with her eyes wide open. When I finished she told me that a friend of hers had been in a motorcycle accident recently. Her friend had survived but she appreciated my story.

The holidays arrived full blown. Decorations, parties, too much to eat and malls crammed with shoppers. I could see joy and celebration all around me. Nonetheless, it was hard for me to feel the spirit of the season. I did my best to paint on a holiday smile; yet, my heart could not be masked. I missed Dion too much. My invisible Christmas list consisted of one thing. Dion back. I knew I could not get what I wanted, but it did not stop me from wanting it.

Journal Entry

I can't believe that it is already December. That just seems crazy to me. Almost 6 months. This year went zooming by, I'm ready for it to go. I'm ready to say "peace out 2006." even though a lot of good things happened this year one event tarnished the relevance of everything else. Everyone's life has moved on and I'm on pause.

How long am I supposed to be still and when will I know when to move on ? I want to write books. I want to counsel people. I want to fall asleep on the beach listening to the waves. I want Dion back. I want to be able to in some way support his family. Someday I want to die and other days I want to live.

2:7 The Awakening of Love

I believe in God but sometimes I feel that He doesn't believe in me.

It's Christmas time and you're not here. Some days your absence hurts worse than other days.

I was all ready to be Mrs. Miller. I miss your smile. I miss how you knew when something was bothering me. You knew me better than just about anybody else. You're gone. And I'm still here on a quest. For what? I don't know. Apparently it is not me that needs something it is God. I just wish you were here in my arms instead of just in my heart and mind.

CHAPTER TWENTY-THREE

Holding On

I bought a daily meditation book, *Healing After Loss Daily Meditations* by Martha Whitmore Hickman. She lost her daughter in a horseback riding accident. She spent part of her mourning process compiling a book of quotes that reflected her understanding of loss.

I looked forward to reading it every day. One of my favorite quotes from her book was, "It is the person we wish to hold on to not the grief." She was right. I wanted to wallow in my grief and not recognize what I was really wanting to hold on to was the man. We would never spend another special day together. That realization alone made my upcoming birthday less exciting because I had looked forward to sharing that birthday with him.

That February 2nd was my birthday. I woke up and noticed that there was something sparkly outside of my window. I opened the blinds to find snow that covered the imperfections of winter just like I wanted my mask to cover my grief. Even though the snow was beautiful, I wasn't too excited about its presence on that day in particular because I had scheduled a small dinner that night. However, I was hoping that my friends had actually planned a surprise party for me and I did not want the weather to ruin that possibility for me. I knew that not too many Nashvillians go out partying in the snow. I had hoped that it would melt by the time my suspected surprise party began.

During the afternoon, one of my friends ventured out in the weather and took me to get a pedicure and manicure. I wore my INSPI(RED)™ shirt from GAP that night hoping to inspire happiness within so that I could get through my "Happy Birthday" without feeling guilty for living and moving on without Dion by my side.

By the time I got to dinner the snow had melted. I was happy about that but not that no surprise party seemed to be in the works. After dinner, I had promised to meet a friend at a nearby lounge. When I got to the lounge, I saw her and made my way through the customers to her side. No sooner had I said hello than a dozen voices shouted "Surprise!"

My brother was there and several of my other friends. I was elated that I had gotten my surprise birthday party. We talked. We laughed. We drank. Some people stayed for just a little while and it seemed that when someone left another person would come. I had a good time. For the first time in a long time, my laughter was not forced. I forgot about my pain and my anger and just immersed myself in my friends and family.

Later that night, I started to sink into my sorrow again. As I climbed into the bed and got under the covers, I realized that Dion had never celebrated my birthday with me and now he never would have the chance to do that. I asked myself and I'm sure others would ask as well, "How can you miss something you never had?" To which I would respond, "Easily."

Dion and I didn't walk down the aisle together at our wedding or feed each other wedding cake. We didn't honeymoon in Tahiti. We didn't get to have his nieces and nephew over so that Jess and Tom could have a night out to themselves. We didn't get to take ballroom dance lessons. There were a million things that we didn't get to do. Could I do these things on my own? Sure except what would be the fun in that. These were supposed to be our moments, not my moments.

It took me so long to even think of wanting to change the "M" to a "W" and go from "Me" to "We." Now he was gone and it hurt like a pain that is unexplainable. The same heart that pumped out blood to keep me alive and alert was the same heart that was broken and aching. For most of the physical pain in our lives we can find a quick fix but there was no magical pill that could make emotional pain just go away. The only things that could quiet that pain were time, patience, trust, hope and love.

That night I dreamt of Dion.

It was night. I was on wooden platform watching a roller coaster careen along the tracks that rose over my head. The wooden scaffolding rocked and swayed as the cars rolled by. Rotted boards groaned along with the music from a carnival calliope. A car pulled into the station. People climbed out, others climbed in but not me. I stood back not even getting close to the cars as people I knew climbed aboard. My mother and father were laughing. Three of my friends climbed in the front car. My brother climbed aboard with a dozen other people I recognized. They were laughing and waving as the car pulled out. I watched from the platform as the line of cars reached the first incline and slowly started cranking up the steep hill.

A hand touched my shoulder. I turned around to discover that Dion was smiling at me. I smiled back. He kissed me and when he pulled back I was surprised at what I saw. We were no longer standing on the platform. We were in the first car climbing a

*hundred feet above the carnival, only feet from the top
and the sheer drop off that followed.*

*My adrenaline was pumping. Someone was screaming,
it might have been me. I looked at Dion, took his
hand in mine and then we were at the top. The car
bucked once. Time enough for one look down. Dozens
of stories below the lights of the carnival glittered like
stars in the Milky Way. I was terrified. Why had I
done this? What was I thinking? I hated roller
coasters. And then we were falling. Toward nothing it
seemed but the tracks caught us and sent the cars
hurtling around sharp corners and through pitch dark
tunnels. Turn by turn I picked up the rhythm of the
ride. I relaxed and found that I loved the experience.
This was the best ride of my life. I saw the faces of
friends and family, proud of me, surprised that I even
got on the roller coaster in the first place.*

*A few more twists and turns and then the ride was
over. Everyone climbed out, laughing and crying. I
turned towards Dion but the car beside me was empty.
He wasn't there. What happened? Where did he go?
Did anyone else notice that he was missing? He was
with me for that one ride but now it was time to go on
and find other adventures without him. But how?
Why would I do that?*

We were supposed to adventure together.

CHAPTER TWENTY-FOUR

Various Forms of Therapy

My father's birthday came a month or so after mine. I told him that I would take him to dinner. I asked him to which restaurant he want to go. In turn, he asked me to which restaurant I wanted to go. It was his birthday, for Pete's sake, so I told him that he should decide. I wanted him to eat at his favorite place on his birthday. After all, I ate at my favorite restaurant for my birthday. Despite my protests, we ended up at the same Japanese restaurant he had taken me to for my birthday.

We had a nice dinner and seemed to be growing closer. I didn't hate him. On the contrary, I loved him. As I worked through my pain, I found it easier to be gentle with him. Yet, I was still a little annoyed that he had let me pick the restaurant for **his** birthday dinner.

The next week at grief counseling, I told Nicole, my therapist, that my father had pretty much coerced me into picking the restaurant for his birthday dinner. To my surprise she got choked up and began to cry. With her voice cracking, she asked me to consider this situation from my father's side. "For his birthday, your father just wanted you to be happy. Your happiness was present enough for him. It had nothing to do with the restaurant; it had to do with the happiness of his daughter."

Her words made me think of the countless gifts he'd given me over the years. Not presents wrapped in paper and bows, but gifts of his time and his wisdom and his patience. Gifts of love. An imperfect human love sure, but one that was steadfast and constant.

I went to bed that night and thanked God for my father and my mother. I thanked God for helping me to grow up a little and see them as people, and to let go of needing them to be perfect. They were doing the best they could considering that they were watching their baby girl grieve and go through one of hardest things that she would ever go through in her life without being able to make it better.

There was a gospel song that says "sometimes you have to encourage yourself." When the choir at my church used to sing that song, I would think, "Wow, that is a lot of pressure."

I remembered the elementary school guidance counselor that I interned with in New York City. She used to say to the children, "Who is the only person that can control your actions?" They would mumble "me" in unison. She would point at them, not harshly but in an empowering way and affirm their answer, "Yes, you."

She used to say the same thing to me from time to time when my own initiative would falter. Remembering these words anchored me to my hopes and desire to give love and so I started to encourage myself. I focused on living in a way that would make Dion smile in heaven. I didn't automatically get happy and started spreading my joy but little by little I did things to help others. I volunteered at the YWCA and worked as a tutor at a local elementary school and I also volunteered with Big Brothers and Big Sisters. I stopped thinking that God took Dion away from me to punish me or that the Devil took Dion away from me to laugh and see me crash and burn.

I knew that Dion had given me so much passion for love and life. I was supposed to live with that same passion.

Together we had come to a new understanding of love and faith and passion and even forgiveness and I was to carry it forward.

I'd come through the darkest part of my grief and I knew that giving up on life wasn't an option. I had a story to tell not only to help heal myself but to help with others who were lost and in pain.

I was ready to go back to work, and the YWCA had a paying position opening up. I applied and they called me for an interview. When I got to the interview two people were sitting at a long rectangular table, a man in front of me and a woman at the head of the table.

The interview started off fairly well. They asked me why I wanted this job. "Why not try to get a job in a school?," the male interviewer asked me.

I told them that I was trying to get my footing back. I'm not sure this was the smart thing to say, however, it was the truth. They asked me what I meant by that. And as if on cue, I began to cry! Right in the middle of the interview. I felt embarrassed, yet I pushed through the sorrow and told them about my short time with Dion. I finished and apologized for my tears. They told me that I need not apologize. The wound was still raw and my emotions were understandable.

I pulled myself together. They asked me a few more questions and we were done. They told me that they would let me know their answer in a few weeks.

"Sure," I thought to myself as I walked away, "Let's hire the inconsolable girl as our counselor."

They called a few weeks later and told me that I didn't get the position. "You are, in our opinion," they said, "overqualified."

I thought to myself that they really meant "overemotional" instead of "overqualified." However, I didn't see this as a setback. I didn't crumble. This experience was just the first step on my journey back to myself.

Looking to rekindle joy and beauty in my life, I changed my MySpace name to AngelatheBeautiful. I even introduced myself as Angela the Beautiful to some people. They would laugh, but I still felt that there was power in that name.

The more I identified with that name, the more I felt like the world was really a beautiful place and that I was one of the beautiful things in it. When I was younger, I used to call my brother conceited and he would say, "I'm not conceited, I'm confident." Now I knew what he meant.

My confidence didn't come from acquiring material things. It came from breaking down the walls that I'd built up around me. It came from wanting to love myself again so that I could learn how to love others.

I was reading more than I ever had in school. Books were no longer scholastic requirements but doorways to new ideas and new experiences. A trip to a Borders book store was like a mini-vacation. I usually stopped in the clearance section to see if anything caught my eye. On one trip, the thinnest book in that section caught my attention. I turned it over in my hand and read the title, A Grief Observed by C.S. Lewis. The front cover was black and white with an image of white roses wilting on a table.

I read the endorsements on the back cover, "Written after his wife's tragic death as a way of surviving..." "Was this some kind of angelic gift from Dion?" I wondered. I bought the book and read it from cover to cover the first night. It was the most amazing seventy six page book I'd ever read. I identified with this man on many levels. He lived in a different time and place from me; and yet, his pain was similar to my own.

Madeleine L'Engle wrote this in the foreword for A Grief Observed, "When C.S. Lewis married Joy Davidman, she was in the hospital. He knew he was marrying a woman who was dying of cancer...his experience of marriage was only a taste...he had been invited to a great feast of marriage and the banquet was rudely snatched away from him before he had done more than taste the hors d'oeuvres."

This book just kept speaking to me. His wife's name had been Joy. They had been married in a hospital. Lewis also questioned God and was angry with God and then he came to a better understanding of God and of himself and of his love for his deceased wife.

I read other books about grief and loss. I released grief and created hope by writing in my journals and writing poetry. I would sit in silence and listen to absolutely nothing which was exactly what I wanted to hear. At other times, I would get caught up in television shows.

One of my favorite forms of therapy was watching the television show, Grey's Anatomy. I identified with one of the characters, Dr. Isobel Stevens, aka Izzy. She had fallen in love with one of her patients. His name was Denny. His character was so charming that I fell in love with him too. At the end of season two, he died suddenly in the hospital just after proposing to her.

The next season began with Izzy lying on her bedroom floor, not wanting to move. Her friends stood outside her door trying to get her to come out, yet she wouldn't budge. I hadn't locked myself in a room, however I had definitely closed myself off from the rest of the world.

Throughout the season, I slowly saw Izzy make progress. At one point she was ready to go back to work. She made it as far as the entrance to the hospital where she lost her nerve. Her friends and colleagues would walk by and prod her to come inside. She'd respond, "Yeah I will be in, go on, I will see you inside." As the hour ended, night had come and Izzy was still standing outside, in the dark, looking up at the hospital.

One of her friends walked to her side and asked, "Where does it hurt?"

I knew exactly where she hurt. It hurt her in the same place that it hurt me. Izzy answered for both of us, "Everywhere."

Izzy slowly recovered and so did I. I knew that I was the only one that could turn my frown around and so I deemed that 2008 was going to be great. I wrote it down in my journal. I told people that it was my goal to make 2008 great. Maybe it sounds corny but it was my way of pulling myself out of the darkness and into new light. I wanted to travel to a place I'd never been before. I was ready to live and enjoy this new and different life. Angela had emerged out of grief.

Journal Entry

I don't know why I'm about to write this but I'm afraid to let Dion go completely. Anne said that maybe I need to forgive somebody. The only person who came to mind was me. I need to forgive myself and the things I did and said before he died and after he died. It's hard to let go of Dion and it's hard to forgive myself. I love Dion and I always will and I know he loves me too. But I've got to try to say goodbye.

Two weeks after Dion died, my good friend Linara's father passed away. He suffered from a rare form of lung cancer which was all the more tragic because he had never smoked. He was an acupuncturist who believed in holistic health. After Dion's funeral, I went to New York to be with Linara and her family.

Near the end of his last night, his daughters gave him tributes, starting with the oldest daughter and moving on to the youngest daughter. They were all heartfelt. The feeling in the room that night was sad, but peaceful. He was a husband, a friend, a father and a doctor and I'm sure that he wore many more hats. One thing that Linara's sister said was, "I know that it is the order of life that the parent must go before the child..."

As I stood there in the room I remembered when I used to visit with Linara and her family. Her father always made time to sit and talk to me. He would make waffles for all of us. He treated me like one of his own daughters. He even tried teaching me some swing dance moves. He was a lot of fun.

While visiting the family at the hospital, I felt a kind of peace or acceptance. I remember Linara's mom looking at me in awe and concern. She asked, "How do you do it? You're scaring me."

I told her that there were many days when I scared myself. I was not sure where my brain was. I was sure I was in a kind of ambulatory shock still from Dion's death, but I knew I wanted to be there for Linara and her family.

I wrote her a letter a little later.

Dear Momma Davidson

I think of you often, I have no words to say,

So instead of calling, I bow my head and pray.

I pray for your strength, I pray for your tears,

I pray for your girls, I pray for the love you shared with him all those years!

I can't say I understand what you're going through but I know it is hard.

So instead of calling you with deafening silence I decided to send this card.

My heart sends out love to you, for I have so much to give. The unfortunate thing about dying is that the grievers have to continue remembering how to live.

I know that God will keep you. He will carry you in his arms.

How do I know that God will keep you? Because he had me to write you this poem!

I love you,

Angela G.

I didn't know it then, but I can see it now. The key to the peace and support I could offer Linara and her family came from feeling my love for them. In time, I was able to move through my own grief by remembering the love Dion and I had created. The love that still lives in me.

By moving through my grief, I had come out on the far side with a greater understanding about ultimate loss. When my aunt, Shirley passed away in late June of 2007, I attended her funeral in Memphis. We got to her house the morning of the funeral. My uncle, her widower, was busy cooking a big breakfast for everyone.

My mother took my father and I aside, "Why would he do that? He should not be worrying about making breakfast?"

My uncle was ready with his answer, "Shirley would have made breakfast for everyone."

My mother started to object. I put my hand on her arm to quiet her. I knew more about grief than my parents at that point. I knew that grief makes you want to feel that the person is still there and so you do things that the other person would have done.

A few nights later, I decided to move the wedding band and engagement ring that I'd been wearing since Dion's passing to my left hand. I moved the wedding band to my right hand. I put the engagement ring on a chain that I wore around my neck. When I moved them, I cried a little, yet it was a necessary step in "moving on."

Journal Entry

I am at a new understanding. It took going to a funeral in Memphis for me to realize that you are far better off in God's hands than you ever were in my hands. I like to think that my arms were pretty good place for you to be. Anyway I listened to the sermon yesterday and it just helped me to realize that if Dion is truly happy that I need not be selfish and should let him go and not keep wishing him back. Not that he could come back.

One year and 20 days after Dion's death, I moved the engagement ring. It was emotional. I didn't have streaming tears just water and my eyes. I took the rings off of my left hand and put them on my right hand. I feel renewed in my loving and living. This is not something that can be so much explained in words but rather felt by my heart. I decided to take the engagement ring and wear it around my neck as a necklace. I keep the wedding band on my right ring finger. I feel good about my decision and the timing of it all. I feel real good. I love you, Dion.

At the end of the summer, I had my last grief counseling session. I was not looking forward to ending my therapy sessions. I'd bonded with Nicole. She had helped me through such a helpless time in my life and for that I would always be grateful. She helped me to see that even though the man that I loved was gone, I was still loving and loved and that I should not give up on falling in love again.

Our last session was at an ice cream parlor. It was hot that day. The air conditioning wasn't working so the ice cream was melting as we talked. In a way I'd become dependent upon our meetings because she was my escape from the rest of life. When I was with her I could stay on pause. I could feel the hurt. I didn't have to wear the mask in those moments that I was confessing my truth to her. In fact, I was happy to take the mask off.

It was hard for me to say goodbye. It felt like the end of a friendship. A friendship I'd known was going to end from the very beginning. She told me that she was proud of me. For my strength and my humor. I told her I could not have made the trip without her. We hugged and said good-bye. As a part of my closure I took a trip to Georgia to visit Dion' family which resulted in the following journal entry.

Journal Entry

I was visiting with Dion's family in Georgia. I was sitting at the table with his niece Amber. She was three at the time and she was playing with some paper, she looked up at me and with sincerity said, "I miss Uncle Dion. Will you take care of him Angela?" My heart melted, "I will."

Jess told me that Amber came to her and Tommy holding candy hearts left over from Valentine's Day.

She must have noticed their sadness because she went to them and placed the candy hearts in the palms of their hands.

"Mom and dad you can use these until you heart is not broken."

Children understand more than we often give them credit for.

"My purpose is far greater than my pain."

-Foxy Brown

CHAPTER TWENTY-FIVE

Pain Into Purpose

That fall I was offered a job at a middle school in Nashville. I was ready to meet the children that were in need of a listening and caring ear. I was ready to turn my pain into purpose.

I'd been there less than three weeks when a seventh grader came crying to me because she'd just lost a friend in a motorcycle accident. Even with my training, and desire to remain objective and in service to this child, within a few moments I was in tears. The student looked confused and I knew I needed to give her some explanation. "I lost my husband to a motorcycle accident." Even as I spoke I wondered if this was the 'right' thing to do, but I just couldn't help myself.

We both cried hard for a while. As she was leaving, I gave her a pencil with roses on it letting her know that my husband had liked to give me roses. So anytime she was down she could look at the pencil and remember that I cared about her well-being.

After she left, I questioned God about his timing. "Really God? I have been here three weeks and you send me a child who has lost someone in a motorcycle accident?" There was no answer, no voice, no explanation and none was needed. I knew that somehow this was part of his plan and I accepted it.

Still, the counselor in me wondered if I had helped her or disturbed her with my own tears. I resolved to do better. "I will not be crying on the job. I cannot break down every time a child comes to me with a heartache." I worked diligently to do just that.

At the end of the school year on the anniversary of Dion's death, the day I called his Angel date, I decided at the last minute that I needed to go somewhere. I was mad at myself because I had known that this date was coming and I'd not started planning for it until the Tuesday before.

I got on the computer and went searching. All I knew was I wanted to go to a beach and the closest beaches were in Florida. Was I ready to go back to Florida? As I was looking, I was praying that the Lord would be with me and help me with my decision.

I found a place called Lauderdale by the Sea that looked good. I'd never been to Ft. Lauderdale before. I booked the trip and told no one of my plans. I didn't want to be stopped nor did I want a traveling companion. I just wanted to be alone and sit on the beach and fall asleep listening to the waves which is how it turned out to be. Long days of nothing pressing to do.

I had the time to reflect on how far I had come, with Dion and then without him. The love I had found with him was still with me. On my last day there, I sat on the beach with a notepad and wrote Dion one last letter.

Dion,

I guess it was all meant to be, you loving me and me loving you. Now you have a new birth date, the day you went to heaven. You have two days that you made the transition into a new life. You know how much I love birthdays and you have two.

I miss you tremendously, that will never stop. Thank you so much for the people that you sent me during this time without you. I know that we will meet again whether it's in my dreams or in heaven. I never stopped loving you once I knew it was love that I was feeling. You changed my life just by loving me for me.

God blessed me with you and I will be forever grateful. When your mother and father came together, they never knew how many lives they would affect by creating you. I'm grateful to them for having you.

Never thought that I would be the one to fall in love but you made me see that was exactly who I needed to be. I loved me with you and I'm learning how to love me without you. It's not easy but I know that it has to be done. You, only and always, just wanted me to be happy. Seems I need help in that area, so stay with me.

Please keep sending me people and signs to show me of your love. I do appreciate them. Help me to recognize them when I'm unsure of what is going on. I still ask God to take care of you because only he can.

I love you Dion and I always will.

Your Angela

"Our prime purpose in this life is to help others. And if you can't help them, at least don't hurt them."

-Dalai Lama

POST SCRIPT

The women's ministry at my church asked me to speak at the Standing on the Promises Tea for the women of the church. There would be about a hundred ladies in attendance. I was to sit on a panel with two other speakers, a female Evangelist and the first lady of my church. I would be the last to speak. I would be following some very strong women from the church. Did they really want me to speak? The woman who approached me was confident that I was the right person so I accepted. Then I had to figure out what I would say..

I didn't want to talk about Dion because I knew that I would probably cry. However, the more I told myself that I didn't want to talk about him, the more my spirit insisted that Dion was what I needed to talk about. This concerned me because my mother would be in the audience. I didn't want to limit what I might say because she would be there, but I didn't want to create even more distance between us either.

As I was preparing for this talk, I kept wondering why they had chosen me to speak. What has God promised me that had come to pass in my life that I could share with other women? I thought of different things that I had prayed for and had received, but nothing that came to mind seemed like the message that I was to give. I asked God to help me say what He wanted me to say.

Over the course of a few days, I wrote a script for my speech. I worked hard on it, putting my best ideas on paper.

The words I wrote told my story, but not my whole truth. The words held my mask in place, protecting me from my emotions.

The morning came and I had my script in hand as I walked to the podium. I placed it on the smooth wooden surface in front of me, looked out at the gathered women, and decided to abandon what I had written and go with my heart. Looking out at the crowd, and at my mother, I began to tell my story.

Two years ago my life changed. I was in love with a man who was taken from me very suddenly. One minute I was on the phone telling him what we were having for dinner and within three hours I received a phone call telling me to go to the hospital immediately. Dion had been in an accident.

As I stood on one side of the hospital bed and the chaplain stood on the other side of the bed he said to me, "even Jesus questioned God from the cross." I know he was trying to let me know that it was okay to ask God, "Why" in times of death. I looked at him and then I looked down at Dion. And I thought, I have nothing to say to God.

When I did finally start talking to God it was out of anger and confusion. I had questions, but I knew that I would not get the answers to them, so what was the point of talking to him.

One morning some months later, the sun was coming through my window and I woke up and began to praise God, but then I realized that I was still mad at him so I stopped. I knew that God was big enough and strong enough to handle my anger, so I didn't feel like I was being disobedient. God knew that I loved him, but more importantly he knew that I was hurting. Anger is just as important an emotion to have and to feel as happiness is.

I wondered how I would be able to go on without Dion. I didn't feel like myself. I felt small and I felt like my grief was an ocean. However, I eventually came to feel that I had a backup generator working for me. The poem Footprints would often pop into my mind. The line that would play over and over again in my heart was, "The times when you see only one set of footprints, it was then that I carried you." In my darkest hours, I would say to myself, God must be carrying me, because I'm not doing this on my own.

It took me some time to get over the shock of losing Dion. It is still hard for me to believe that he is not here with me physically. But because I opened up my heart, I knew that some kind of purpose would have to result from all the pain that I was feeling.

I still miss and love Dion greatly, but I know that I have more love to give. So I try to remember to give love in all that I do. Mother Theresa said do ordinary things with extraordinary love. I'm learning that truth day by day.

As a guidance counselor I wish I could help and heal every problem that walks through my door but I have realized that I will not be able to solve the problem of every child. However, it is my job to assist the child in his or her emotional and academic development. I have spoken with men and women in the counseling profession as well as the teaching profession and they often feel as though they are not reaching the children. I tell them that as long as they are doing the best they can that is all that matters. The truth is that we never really know how far our words and wisdom travel with the children that we serve. I learned that from a seventh grader.

I had always viewed tears as a sign of weakness. I never wanted anyone else to see me as weak. And then Dion helped me see that crying was okay and even good for me. During my first weeks as a counselor, a child came to me who had just lost a friend in a motorcycle accident. As she told me her story, I broke down and we cried together. I told her my story about losing Dion and I gave her a pencil to remember that I loved her whenever she felt alone. She smiled and left. I worried that I had acted unprofessionally. I feared that I'd done as much damage as good.

2:7 The Awakening of Love

I wondered each day until the end of the school year when she found me in the hallway. She smiled at me and then put a note in my hand:

> Hey Ms. Grant,
>
> U know u are my favorite guidance counselor ever. I appreciate u for being there for me now. I know I can count on u to be there. I enjoyed the times we shared especially the first time when we was both crying. Well I hope to c u next year. Love you lotz.

As I finished speaking, tears were streaming down my face. I was not embarrassed by them. I didn't feel weak because of them. I had earned them. As I stepped from the podium, I was greeted with hugs and congratulations. One of the last hugs I got was from my mother. I cannot say if she had been crying along with me as I spoke, but her hug said clearly that she was with me now. We love imperfectly perhaps, but permanently.

As we closed the ceremony that day, we joined hands and sang a song I knew well. The same song that was sung at Dion's funeral, His Eye is on the Sparrow.

"I sing because I am happy, I sing because I am free,

His eye is on the sparrow and I know he watches me."

Spring had come. The sun was out and the sky was a blazing shade of blue. As I pulled away from the parking lot, I switched on the radio. A song by Erykah Badu came through the speakers. The lyrics were about the baggage and issues that women carry around with them. She sang for us to let them go.

"I guess nobody ever told you all you must hold on to is you. Let it go, let it go, let it go, let it go."

The song is saying let go of the hurt. Let go of the excuses that you have made for yourself. Let go of the pain of the past.

I listened until she got to the bridge, my favorite part of the song. With a smile on my face, I started to sing along.

> *"I betcha love can make it better, I betcha love, I betcha love can make it better…"*

I sang at the top of my lungs. I know from my own life that she is right. Love can and will make it better.

I live in spite of my grief and the pain of losing Dion knowing that loving him was a part of my purpose in life, and part of a bigger broader picture that I was not aware of until now.

I have come to the conclusion that when God takes something away he does offer you something better. A better understanding of who you are through the triumph as well as tribulation. A better understanding of life and of love.

The sweetest thing I have ever known was love and it will continue to be the sweetest thing I will ever know. And love WILL make it better!

2:7 The Awakening of Love

ABOUT THE AUTHOR

Angela Aileen Grant is a licensed school counselor, entrepreneur, and author. Her name means "messenger who sheds great light" which is what she has devoted her life to doing in her writing and her work.

Angela received her B.A. in Early Childhood Education from Clark Atlanta University in Atlanta, Georgia and her M. A. in Applied Psychology specializing in K-12 Counseling and Guidance from New York University.

Angela was born and raised in Nashville, TN where she currently resides. She enjoys traveling, spending time with family and friends, and cooking and eating good food. Angela knows that she is blessed to be a blessing. Therefore, she recognizes, appreciates and values each day encouraging others along the way.